Life Skills for Young Adults

How to Survive Each Day and the Rest of Your Life

International English Edition

Philip J. Cassidy

BALBOA.
PRESS

A DIVISION OF HAY HOUSE

2013 concept by Philip Cassidy.
First published in Australia 2014
Cover Design and Internal Artwork by Michael John Lewis.

Balboa Press books may be ordered through booksellers or by contacting:

Balboa Press
A Division of Hay House
1663 Liberty Drive
Bloomington, IN 47403
www.balboapress.com
1 (877) 407-4847

Comments and Enquiries can be made to the author at www.teentoadult.com

Print information available on the last page.

ISBN: 978-1-4525-2778-9 (sc)
ISBN: 978-1-4525-2779-6 (e)

Balboa Press rev. date: 03/18/2015

Introduction

Congratulations on reaching adulthood You made it. I wish you all the best that life and love has to offer, but at this stage of your life you need to remember that you are not 'bulletproof' and you do not know everything. People your age die every day, are living with serious illnesses and are struggling to make it in this world.

So where do you go from here? For some young adults the path may be easier because they currently have a job, they are going to university or into the military. Unfortunately for many other young adults, leaving school and home can be a confusing time.

This book is designed to give you tips and information on how to find your way through life and how to get the most out of your new independence. It is a big, unforgiving world out there that requires money, safety, luck, timing, health, other people's help and a lot of other skills to successfully get through each day.

These tips and lessons have stood the test of time over the decades but may not wholly apply to your current situation so this book must be treated as a ***general guide only*** because circumstances will be different for each person.

The main aims of this book are to get you to think with your brain, not get caught up in the emotion of the moment, push you to do your own research, seek professional advice where necessary and ask the right questions, so that you will save time and money in order to provide the best possible life for yourself, future partner and children. The more informed you are the fewer mistakes you should make. **As it is often said... Knowledge is Power.**

So many doubts are probably entering your mind about what to do now because maybe you don't have a plan and don't know how to get started, so there are chapters especially devoted to those processes for you.

Dedication

To my Parents, Sister and Guardians.

And...to all the people around the world who are working tirelessly to give the elderly, the disabled, the disadvantaged and disengaged young adults in their community comfort, support, purpose and direction. You do not receive the thanks you deserve.

Acknowledgements

The author wishes to acknowledge the contribution of the following people through their support and assistance in the production of this book. With any project you need a team of people that can deliver certain qualities in order to reach your goal.

Tania Wilmot and Rebecca Clemas BSc (contributing writers), Shona Mackay, Aaron Souter (graphic and web design), Shannon Sciuto (business and accounting), Mike Shearer and Matilda Elliot (additional material and editing) Michael Harding (editing), Brendon Woolley (technical support), Michael Hickey, Greg Wheatley, Michael John Lewis (artwork), Ela Kiesel, Tully Skinner, Lachlan Jones, Sandi van Barneveld, Lisa Lyford and the Mackay & Dyer families.

About the Author

I was born in a small New Zealand town. My mother died when I was four. My younger sister and I were brought up by my father until he died the week before sitting my Year 10 exams. I estimate that I shifted house 16 times in my life before I left home to join the Navy. I chose the medical profession where I discovered in myself the quality of empathy and a desire to give great customer service.

But I was young and so unaware of how to look after myself. The Navy provided job security and a place to live but I knew nothing about real world aspects like tax, retirement plans, budgeting, buying a car or signing documents. I had no adult role model in my life that I felt I could turn to. I made a lot of mistakes that cost me time and money and now want to pass on to today's young adults what I have learned through my experiences.

From the time I left the Navy in 1990 I estimate I have had over 30 different employments throughout Australia, NZ and the United Kingdom. Many of the qualifications such as Nursing, Occupational Health and Safety and Security Operations have been achieved late in life. I have also developed a current patent on a sports management system.

I have lived in Australia since 2002 where I have been employed as a Tour Guide as well as being involved with transporting and working with disabled children. For the past 3 years I have been looking after an elderly lady on a part time basis, who has no family of her own in the city.

The Author of this book has made a lot of Mistakes

Yes the person who wrote this book, throughout his life has made a lot of mistakes. Some really big ones…I suffered from a period of depression as a result of a lot of my mistakes building up, *BUT* learning from those mistakes has got me to where I am today. This book for all its information, tips and life lessons older people have learned, will not prevent you from making your own mistakes, but aims to make you *'THINK BEFORE YOU ACT'* so that you limit your mistakes to *SMALL* ones.

Writing This Book

The idea for this book began from the simple idea of wanting to give my nieces and nephew some information and lessons in life I had learned. I wanted to give them a 'head start' in life in order to save them time and money when they left home. School teaches you many things but it does not teach you many of the skills that you need, to handle day to day life once you leave school or move out of home.

I knew I had a great idea and everyone I talked to agreed, but without any action this book was *ONLY* going to be a dream. I started researching famous people to find out how they became successful. The common thing they were all saying was, if you have a talent, a vision or an idea, you are going need the right people around you to make it happen. You cannot do it on your own. You need the right people to work for you, guide you and mentor you.

All through the process of producing this book, I believe there has been more than an ounce of heavenly intervention. I don't know how else to explain it. I have been incredibly lucky at times with thoughts 'popping up' at the right time, being in the right place and finding the right people to help me. Those people shared my passion and are doing great things in the community already, but the frustrating thing for me as a writer is, they are busy people. Until we could have a meeting all I could do was try to ask the right questions and form a basic plan on the direction to take so I could keep moving towards my goal.

While writing this book I still had to earn money to survive. I had three casual jobs (school bus driver, pub tour driver and pizza delivery driver) as well as being a Community Carer. One lesson right there; Do what you have to do in order to get where you want to be.

Disclaimer (Caveat)

Simple Version

This book contains information, tips and lessons learned from the author's extensive experience and own mistakes in the course of his day to day life, as well as those of other sources (the "Information"). The Information is to be used as a reference only, as it is an indication of the timing and circumstances experienced by the author and sources at the time of occurrence and may not wholly apply to your current situation.

In any event, you should always seek the opinions of your parent(s), adult role models in your life, government departments, of professionals in their particular field and conduct your own research. The Information must not be relied upon and is not intended as financial, accounting, legal, medical or other such specialist advice and you must obtain specialist professional advice in respect of such matters.

This edition of the book has been adapted from the original version (Australia and New Zealand). It contains information that is still relevant to your lifestyle however the information is deemed **'general in nature'** and will require you to do some research on how things are actually done in your particular country. You have the ability within yourself to find information, people and organisations in your local area to help you, by looking in your phone book or going online into your favourite 'search engine' and entering key word(s).

Disclaimer

The Legal Version

The author shall not be liable for any actions, claims, liability, loss, damage or injury sustained in connection with or arising from the use of the Information, howsoever such loss, damage or injury may arise or be caused, including but not limited to, the author's negligence, act, omission, breach of contract, breach of statutory duty or otherwise. You acknowledge that all Information is provided on a non-specific, generic basis only.

Under the applicable State, Provincial and Commonwealth Laws of your country (including, without limitation the Competition and Consumer Acts ("CCA"), certain statutory implied guarantees and warranties (including, without limitation the statutory guarantees under the CCA) may be implied (Non-Excluded Guarantees). The author acknowledges that nothing herein purports to modify or exclude the Non-Excluded Guarantees. Except as expressly set out herein or in respect of the Non-Excluded Guarantees, the author makes no warranties or other representations including but not limited to the quality or suitability of the Information. The author's liability in respect of these warranties is limited to the fullest extent permitted by law

How To Use This Book

There is too much information in this book for you to try and read it in the usual way. It is best to consider this book as a *reference* book. With a problem or situation in your life there may be an answer or direction available under an applicable chapter amongst these pages.

What I have written is to be classed as *a general guide only* but by thinking before you act, doing some research yourself, planning as much as you can and asking the right questions of the right people, you will be close to the right answers for most situations in your life.

Also, I really want you to talk to an adult role model that you have in your life and try and find the balance between what they suggest, what I have written, what your research has told you and what you feel is the intelligent way to approach any problem you may have.

Stay Strong and Good Luck

Contents

Health

Relationships

Travel

Things Are Not as They Seem

The Top Tips

Life and all that...

Rules of Life

These "Rules of Life" have been accredited to Bill Gates, the founder of Microsoft, in a speech he [never] gave at a high school in the U.S. They were originally published by Charles J. Sykes in a book titled "50 Rules Kids Won't Learn in School."

1. Life is not fair, get used to it.
2. The world does not care about your self esteem. The world will expect you to accomplish something *before* you feel good about yourself.
3. If you think your teacher is tough, wait till you get a boss.
4. Flipping burgers is not beneath your dignity. Your grandparents had a different word for burger flipping…they called it 'opportunity'.
5. You will not make $100 000 a year (40 000 originally) right out of high school. You won't be a vice president with a company credit account.
6. If you mess up it is not your parents fault so don't whine about your mistakes. Learn from them and move on.
7. Before you were born your parents weren't as boring as they are now. They got that way from paying your bills, cleaning your clothes and listening to you talk about how cool you are. So before you save the rainforest from the parasites of your parent's generation, try delousing the closet in your own room.
8. Your school may have done away with winners and losers but life has not. In some schools they have abolished failing grades and they will give you the test as many times as you need to pass. This doesn't bear the slightest resemblance to anything in real life.
9. Life is not divided into semesters. You don't get the summer off and very few employers are interested in you finding yourself. Do that on your own time.
10. Television is not real life.
11. Be nice to nerds. Chances are you will end up working for one.

General Information

Life is not easy

Believe it when we say "You have had it very easy so far." With all the war and hunger going on elsewhere in the world, you have had a great life. You have probably been given a very good education by world standards, had a roof over your head, and probably not had to go hungry for more than a day. When you leave home, you will have to survive on your own.

There are *NO* guarantees when living your life

There are no guarantees of success, happiness, riches, a long life, romance or constant employment. To make the *BEST* decisions ask questions, do the research and get as informed as you can. You should be thinking a bit more about things before you grab opportunities or take chances.

The most important goal in life should be happiness and peace of mind

If you are constantly being stressed out, your health, relationships and job will suffer. Try and keep your life as organised and as simple as possible so that you have some energy to tackle the difficult times.

Life should be about the QUALITY of your time

Everybody gets *exactly* the same number of hours in every year. People who enjoy quality of life are those people who have learned that how they use their time, is much more important than how much they own. Use your income and possessions wisely to make your time more enjoyable, not to impress others.

YOUR 'PAUSE BUTTON' (This is VERY Important)

Before you do anything that can damage yourself, other people or your bank account, you need to *STOP* and think about what you are about to do and how it will impact your life if it doesn't work out. You may need to ask more questions, do more research, get another opinion from someone you trust or take some time to go over documents *before* you sign them. A common saying is; "Second thoughts are often best." Your 'pause button' is your safety net.

Most of the knowledge you learned at school won't be used once you leave

What you *did* learn was how to read, write, spell, and do maths. If you got a qualification that's great. Pretty much everything else was teaching you *how to think,* and *how to find information.* Eventually you will see it's benefits.

Your education does not stop when you have left school

You are in life's classroom now and she is an unpredictable beast just waiting to knock you down. You will have 'bad' days like everyone else. Remember there is always someone in your community having a worse day than you and that tomorrow is another day. The decisions and choices that you have made in your life make up the person you are today.

Have a thirst for knowledge

Gaining knowledge can give you a feeling that you are uncovering some of life's secrets that not everyone knows.

You will learn something new every day

It may be about you, someone else, general knowledge or a new skill but you will learn something new.

"There is nothing so costly as ignorance" Horace Mann

If you have plenty of money and plenty of time then this does not apply to you. Thinking that you do not need anyone's help or advice is going to slow your success and cost you time and money.

You will benefit a lot if you plan and organise your life

By planning and organising you will keep your life a lot simpler, which means less stress. Stress can harm your relationships with people.

Have a day planner (with times) to map out busy days and prioritise your work

This will help you organise your life. Writing things down means appointments aren't missed, phone calls are made and you can keep track of your money etc.

Most things in life require more thought, time, energy and money than you first imagined

This book for example, started from a simple idea. I had 90% of the information in the first four months but it took another 365 days to design the covers, talk and meet with the right people, promote the idea, edit the content, find the email addresses and phone numbers of over 3000 schools in Australia, contact them, design the website, organise the printing, set up a small business and get the books delivered on time to those schools that ordered them.

To seek the answers you need, you *MUST ASK* the *RIGHT* questions...*EVERYTIME*

This is a skill that takes a while to master. Take time to think about the answer you want and build the question to get that answer. There is no point dropping hints hoping the person will pick up what you are wanting. Ask the right question(s).

Never be afraid to ask questions, or ask for help and assistance

Recognising when to ask for help can save you time and money.

When you share a problem, you halve a problem

Talking to someone and unloading a problem can be a weight off your shoulders...and they may have an answer.

Two (or more) heads are better than one

A few brains working on the same problem usually come up with the right answer.

You wanted your independence.
You are now considered an adult.
It is time to take responsibility for your actions.

Always think *SAFETY*

Consider, if you are injured how will that affect your life? Who will look after you, who will pay your bills? Any insurance cover you may have for loss of income may only pay about 75% of your average income over the past 6-12 months. Put a bit simpler it means you may have to survive on three quarters of the money you are used to receiving. Any government sickness or disability payment you may be entitled to, will only allow you to barely survive. It is going to be a lot easier if you just think about the safety aspects before you act.

The degree of your injury (to yourself or your bank account) is directly related to what degree you under-estimated the risk.

Even if you do minimal research or planning, you won't do as much damage as if you have done no research at all.

Promises define your character

If you can't keep them, don't make them.

Actions speak louder than words

Talk is cheap. Rather than talking up something, try going out and doing it and people will take you much more seriously. Anyone can talk, but only a few back up their words with action.

Cherish every moment of your life as special

In a split second, your life can be gone.

Be true to your heart (what you believe in)

Do what you know in your heart is right – trust your instincts.

Your fantasies are perfect, reality is not

Bad people, bad timing, bad weather, breakdowns and stress all make that idea of the perfect moment turn into something less than perfect.

Being in the right place at the right time helps open up opportunities

This happens occasionally. Somehow you've created your own luck and you were in the right place at the right time to take an opportunity you needed.

Good luck happens as does bad luck

You will have days when you think the 'planets have aligned' and it is 'your' day. You can't do a thing wrong. Cherish these days because they are rare. The occasions when everything 'turns to custard' happen far more often where you feel you just want to go home and climb back into the comfort and safety of your bed and start a new day tomorrow.

Things may happen for a reason

When bad things happen it can be hard to reason why it should be happening to you at this moment. The reason may not become clear until years later but it will have made you stronger. When good things happen, I tell myself I am a good person and I deserve it.

Be careful what you wish for.

This is a classic piece of advice handed down through the ages. When you get what you wished for, it usually brings its own set of problems.

Variety is the spice of life, mix it up

Occasionally change something in your life. It could work out better for you.

Life can take you from the highest of highs to the lowest of lows in a short space of time

It can be unbelievable how quickly the best feeling one minute can become a very bad day the next.

If you have a talent

Train to develop it and see how far it takes you. Refer to 'Secrets of Successful People.'

Do a small business course

If you have an inventive or creative mind, are one of life's 'go getters' or eventually want to be your own boss, then a small business course will put you on the right track to success.

Talk to those people you trust, about anything in this book
Get a variety of opinions and advice. It opens up lines of communication and while people may not agree with everything that is written in this book, you'll get to hear different opinions and make up your own mind what direction to take.

Seek inspiration from other people's stories and experiences
There are plenty of books, usually known as biographies, written by or about people you admire, that tell you where they started and how their life changed.

If it sounds 'Too Good To Be True', it *usually* is
Investment opportunities are presented by 'slick' sales people. Realise that they may put pressure on you to 'get in now while the market is hot.' Hit your pause button. Ask questions. Walk away and do your research. Work out the truth. A couple more days are not going to matter.

"Democracy is not a spectator sport, it's a participatory event. If we don't participate in it, it ceases to be a democracy" Michael Moore
Use your voice to speak out against bad government policies. The government should be working for the people's best interests.

"It is not the function of our government to keep the citizen from falling into error: it is the function of the citizen to keep the government from falling into error."
Robert H Jackson, Chief U.S prosecutor Nuremberg Trials, Berlin 1945
When the government starts becoming out- of -control and limiting the rights and liberties of it's citizens, it is up to those citizens to let the government know their actions will not be tolerated.

The only thing necessary for the triumph of evil is for good men to do nothing Edmund Burke
If you stand aside and let people abuse your rights, what is it going to take before you do something about it? Complain, write letter's, protest, but you should *DO* something.

Know your rights and stand up for them

Your 'civil liberties' (basic human rights) are being eroded by your local authority, police, and governments every day. Just because something is done and is accepted as normal (the 'status quo'), it doesn't mean that it is legal or morally acceptable. Examples to research are traffic fines, real estate agents and the bad side of auctions.

Never be afraid to complain about bad service or a product

If you are not happy with the treatment you are given you should firstly complain to the person responsible, or their manager. Be very careful complaining on 'facebook' or other social media, because even though your dissatisfaction could be quite valid it could backfire on you in future, such as when you apply for jobs, or even lead to legal problems. Go online and search for "consumer rights".

Changes to your life and routine

Changes are sometimes forced upon us by a variety of factors. I believe changes outside of our control happen for a reason. Change prevents us from being lazy in activity and thought and brings new challenges. Try to adapt to them.

Nice people *CAN* and *DO* finish 'last'. Use your voice and stand up for yourself.

It can take years to get the confidence to stand up for yourself.

When I left home at 17, I had people taking advantage of my good nature for years. I had friends asking for money and not paying it back. I was getting ripped off by salespeople. I was about 32 when I said to myself "no more." I was finding my voice, the desire to seek knowledge and trying to ask the right questions so I would not be taken advantage of again.

Know your limits

Be realistic about your strengths, weaknesses and capabilities.

Act on your adventurous spirit

Your mind and body is young and full of adventure. Assess the risks to your safety, take the right precautions and go for it.

Be proactive not reactive
Being *proactive* means thinking about the challenges ahead and taking action before they become a problem. Being *reactive* means waiting for the day the challenge arrives and then doing something about it. That usually puts you under more pressure and you tend to make mistakes because you didn't prepare for it.

Dealing with ANY task
Take time to think about what you need to do to get the right result.
Concentrate on the task at hand.
Break big tasks into a number of smaller tasks.
Ask the right questions when unsure about something.

Always seek the *RIGHT ADVICE* when unsure
It is better to seek the advice of professional people than to go it alone. There may be a small cost to pay initially, but that advice could end up saving you thousands of dollars and a lot of time.

Never put off until tomorrow, what you can do today Thomas Jefferson
It is very easy to say to yourself 'It can wait till tomorrow.' I find tomorrow becomes busy, the weather changes or something comes up that's more important. If you have the time, do it today.

Lend a helping hand in your community and give back to society
This could be through a number of community organisations, it doesn't need to be a lot of time, just a couple of hours each week is sufficient. You'll find it not only helps others but you'll get a really great feeling inside. (It will also look good on your CV when you apply for jobs!)

No matter how bad your day is going, there is always someone in your area having a worse one than you
Yeah, you are having a bad day, but there is someone in your neighbourhood going cold, going hungry or losing their self worth.

Try to leave this world a better place for the next generation
Donate clothes to a homeless shelter, volunteer at a charity three or four times a year, sponsor a child, look at organisations in your community that care for the land, animals, forests, rivers and oceans and see how you can help.

Don't volunteer to do just anything on the spur of the moment

Until you are fully aware of what is required and the dangers or risks involved. This is something I learned from being in the military.

DESPITE ALL THESE RECOMMENDATIONS, YOU WILL MAKE YOUR OWN MISTAKES

You need to learn from your mistakes and try to 'bounce back. Chances are it is 'not the end of the world.' Don't give up...try and find positive aspects in bad situations. Next time you will probably just need to think a bit more before you act (see the paragraph 'Your Pause Button' at the start of this chapter).

Trust has to be earned. You should not give that away.

Trusting someone before you know them leaves you open to disappointment and probably less money in your pocket or bank account.

"It is better to offend someone by saying NO, than to fight someone because you said YES too soon." Neil Jenman

Lending money to someone is a good example. They have had plenty of time to pay it back but *YOU* feel bad asking for it.

As you get older, spend time with family and relatives

It should not be only weddings and funerals that bring the family together.

Do unto others as you would have them do unto you

There's another way of putting this: don't do to others what you don't want anyone to do to you. Treat others as you expect to be treated. Most people I talked to put this at the top of the list of important advice to give you.

Don't do mean things to people who can't afford it or don't deserve it

Be a good person and help the less fortunate in your society.

Give elderly people a helping hand

A great injustice in this world is how we treat the elderly people in our society. They are not given dignity, respect and appreciation by much of the modern generation. Your parents sacrificed a lot for you to survive. Say thank you occasionally and look after them when they are old. You will expect the same from your children.

School friends
The friends you had at school are entering a new stage of their lives just like you and unless you are going to work together, you will not see much of each other because your goals will be different. Try to stay in contact with each other and get together occasionally.

Emergency information for the people in your household
In case of emergency, your local emergency phone number will put you in contact with the Fire, Police and Ambulance Service. They will require certain information especially *YOUR EXACT LOCATION*. The ambulance service need to know about medication, medical conditions and allergies that the patient has, to be able to give them the right treatment quickly in order to save their life. Your parents probably know your information *BUT* do you know theirs? Ask them to write it down so *you* can save **their** life.

Be prepared for disasters
This includes **Food, Clothing, Water, Transport, Shelter, Torch, Radio, Batteries**. Bad weather can cut power for days but you usually get plenty of warnings it is on its way. Earthquakes for example can be instant. You don't need to be a 'doomsday prepper', but it helps to have a back-up plan that includes escape routes and enough supplies in case of any natural disaster.

A major accident is not caused by a single mistake
Accidents where planes crash, ships sink, and buildings fall down, all happen because a lot of little mistakes happened along the way. Nothing was done about them and they all came together to cause one major problem. Any mistakes you *DON'T* report may have a serious result at a later date. Don't assume that "they'll already know" or "somebody else will already have told them". *REPORT THEM YOURSELF.*

Donate to Charity

You are probably thinking that you don't have enough for yourself so how can you possibly be thinking of giving any away? Well, this chapter is here because if you develop an attitude of thinking about others and doing what you can when you can, no matter how little, you will find that you become a much happier person than if you only ever think about yourself. This has been proven by experts over and over again.

You are very *LUCKY*. The fact that you live in an established or developing country should give you an appreciation of the quality of life you have grown up with. Always try to remember that there are people in this world who are a lot happier with less than you have. I know that life is a struggle to survive on a daily basis but please, throughout your life whenever you have a few dollars or even spare change, please give it to any charity which is trying to make the world a better place. Your help for those who need a hand doesn't have to be money, it can be some of your time.

I encourage you to choose one or two charities that you feel you would like to help on occasion throughout your life. Any spare time or money that you have will be greatly appreciated and it does give you a great feeling when you make a contribution and, although we cannot save the world on our own, we can still make a difference in someone's life.

NOTE: Not all the money that you give to a charity goes to those in need. Non-profit organisations usually have to cover a lot of costs such as looking after their volunteers, transport, running an office, advertising, insurances and so on. You may want to contact the charity and ask them the actual percentage of donations that get to the people they help or for the services they provide.

The Environment

You need to take some *TIME* to *THINK* about how *YOUR* actions can have an effect on the environment.

YOURS is the generation that needs to leave the state of the Earth for your children and future generations, in a better condition. I know that generations of people before you have taken the earth's resources and changed the landscape for their own needs in order to have a better life, business or product **(where there is profit to be made, there is greed)** but *YOURS* is the generation that needs to think more about how to slow down or stop damage happening in your area.

There are so many different landscapes within our environment which all need to be healthy. These are the swamps, the rivers, the deserts, the seas, the mountains and even our backyards. Every one of the native plants and animals in those landscapes (biodiversity) has a purpose for being there, whether as part of the food chain or to support the area in its own way. It is important that these plants and animals stay healthy in order for their own community to operate as efficiently as possible.

But environments all over the world are changing – and not for the best. One major theory is that too much carbon dioxide (CO_2) is being released into the atmosphere from burning coal and oil. Basically the CO_2 is like a blanket covering the earth trapping heat and making the climate more extreme and very unstable. The ice caps are melting, storms and droughts have increased in severity as well as bringing harsher summer and winter temperatures. Of major concern is that our wildlife cannot adapt fast enough to live with these quick changes. The vegetation changes with the differing temperatures, as well as the animals within that landscape. Climate Change is one of the major threats to our biodiversity.

Also of concern is the human population increasing at such a rate that in the future we do not know how the world will feed everyone, let alone the damage it will cause to the environment. We can already see the damage humans unthinkingly create in our 'own backyards' through over-fishing, the careless use and disposal of chemicals, the introduction of non-native 'pests' and land clearance etc.

These are just a few of the factors that are causing the decline of our environment. Your area of the planet needs to be healthy in order to have the quality of air you breathe, food you eat and water you drink.

Less pollution and a healthier environment means our health will be better and less money needs to be spent on cleaning up the damage/impact? As government budgets become increasingly tight, less and less money will be available for environmental issues, yet so much needs to be done. It is up to *YOU* and your generation to do as much as you can for the environment around your home, work, and local area. Communities will need to make sure the collective voice of the people bring the important environmental issues to government's attention. It should not wait until a problem develops before anyone does anything about it.

If we as individuals can change the small things, and use our collective consumer power to get governments and corporate companies to change the big things, then we can make a difference. By helping the environment you are helping yourself, the ones you love and the family you are yet to meet. Remember we share this precious Earth.

What we must all now do is control how we live our day to day life, and the choices we make that affect the environment we live in.

- Never litter and at the ABSOLUTE MINIMUM you should be recycling. Recyclable material DOES NOT go in the rubbish bin.
- Reduce the amount of driving you do. Buy a bike or take public transport. You will feel better for the exercise and save petrol.
- Get involved in a volunteer environmental organisation. Meet new people and increase your skills.
- Upgrade your electronic devices only when they no longer suit your needs. Don't get pulled by peer pressure or marketing to get the latest new thing.
- Bulk buy your high use items to save money and less packaging.
- Shop at 'opportunity' and second hand stores to save money.
- Grow your own vegetables or buy organic items.
- Spread the word to be responsible about the environment.

Go on-line and search for '50 ways to help the planet'

In Your Own Country
Please go online and search for environmental organisations in your local area.
There will be many organisations trying to help manage environmental issues
regarding the plants, soil, wildlife, rivers and oceans.

Please make some time (it does not have to be a lot) and volunteer to help out.
You will meet like-minded people and you will have a great feeling knowing
you have made a contribution to your community.

Thank You.

Your Human Rights

Human Rights recognise the value that each person has, regardless of where they come from, what has happened in their past and what they believe. Those rights aim to encourage everyone to treat each person with dignity, mutual respect and equality.

Each country in the world has a different way of looking at Human Rights and only some of the recommended rights of people may be given while other rights may be ignored.

If you have ever watched the news on TV you will no doubt have heard and seen examples of Human Rights abuses in countries all over the world. The most graphic of these abuses seem to occur in countries that generally do not have a stable government, have been affected by war or are extremely poor.

Even in 'Western' societies such as Australia, New Zealand, South Africa, Europe, England the USA and Canada etc, the citizens of those countries can also experience abuse of their human rights but in a much less dramatic fashion.

After the tragic display of human rights violations during World War II a 'foundation' document that is known as the Universal Declaration of Human Rights was drawn up and it was adopted by the United Nations in 1948. Note that not all countries belong to the United Nations General Assembly. The Declaration of Human Rights has formed the basis of many human rights treaties across the world. Examples of these treaties are;

- The International Covenant on Civil and Political Rights
- The International Covenant on Economic, Social and Cultural Rights
- The Convention on the Elimination of All Forms of Racial Discrimination
- The Convention on the Elimination of All Forms of Discrimination against Women
- The Convention Against Torture and Other Cruel, Inhuman or Degrading Treatment or Punishment
- The Convention on the Rights of the Child
- The Convention on the Rights of Persons with Disabilities.

192 countries (out of 196) have agreed to these treaties by signing them, also spoken of as 'ratifying' them.

So what are some of your rights as a human being?

It depends where you live but generally speaking some or all of the following may apply to you:

1. Every person is born free and has equal dignity and rights.
2. Every person is allowed all of the human rights without being discriminated against based on their religion, race, colour, age, sex, country or opinion.
3. Every person has a right to live with freedom and safety.
4. No-one has any right to own us nor can we own a person.
5. Every person has a right *NOT* to be subjected to torture, cruel or inhuman punishment or treatment.
6. The law must recognise everyone as a person.
7. We are all protected by the law. The law is the same for everyone. It must treat everyone fairly.
8. Every person has a right to seek corrective action when their human rights have been violated.
9. Each person shall be free from arrest and holding without cause and transfer to another place.
10. The right to a fair trial. Any trial needs to be done publicly. We have the right to a lawyer to represent us. The person(s) judging us must be able to do so without bias or discrimination and must not be directed by anyone else regarding their decision.
11. Innocent until proven guilty. Each person has a right to be presumed innocent. It is up to others to *PROVE* whether you are guilty.
12. Each persons home, family, privacy,honour and reputation shall not be harmed without good reason.
13. Each person has the right to move and live within the confines of their country, within the limits of freedom and rights of others.
14. Every person has a right to asylum in another country away from persecution unless they have been involved in criminal activity or war crimes.
15. Every person has a right to belong to a country (nationality).

16. Each person of correct (full) age has a right to marry and have a family so long as there is full and individual agreement between the couple.

17. Each person has a right to own one or more properties either by themselves or with others and not have that property taken from them without good cause.

18. We all have the right to believe in whatever we want; to believe in and practice our chosen religion and to change our mind, thoughts, conscience and religion if we want to.

19. We all have the right to say what we think and to share our ideas with people in whatever form we choose.

20. Everyone has the right to gather together as a peaceful group. No one can be forced to join a group

21. Every person can be a representative of their country or has a right to elect their representative (vote). The government's authority lies with the will of the people.

22. Every person has the right to government benefits to ensure their personal dignity and personal development.

23. Everyone has the right to choose the type of work they are employed in and that the conditions of their work are fair and just. They have a right to equal pay for equal work and to form or belong to a trade union to protect their workers rights.

24. Everyone has the right to have adequate time away from work to rest and relax, not to have long working hours and to have paid holidays.

25. Every person has the right to an adequate standard of living for themselves and their family. This includes food, water, healthcare, accommodation and social services. Special care and assistance entitlements are given to mother and child.

26. Everyone has the right to education. Early and fundamental education shall be free. Education is designed to develop the human personality and encourage the promotion of peace through tolerance, understanding and friendship. Parents have a right to choose the type of education they want for their children.

27. Every person has the right to enjoy the cultural life of their community and to benefit from the advances in technology. Every person who is the original producer of scientific advancement, artistic work and literature has protection rights (copyright) of their moral and material interests.

28. Every person is entitled to a system whereby their complaints about rights and freedom abuses can be fully determined.
29. Every person is encouraged to actively participate in their community to realise full personal development.
30. The rights laid out in the United Nations Declaration may not be used by any country, organisation or person who wish to destroy the rights and freedoms accorded to every person.

Human Rights in YOUR Country

This is where you will have to do some research yourself to find out exactly which Human Rights are recognised by the government of your State, Province or Country. Go online and look under 'rights and freedoms'

There may also be a government department in your country called the Human Rights Commission. Find out what their role is and what services they provide.

Getting Set Up

I Don't Have a Plan

The Grades you got in School *DO NOT* dictate the rest of your life
People including employers will soon stop caring about your school grades
once you have one or two Letters of Recommendation (references) and be
much more interested in how you are doing *now*.

Don't have a plan? You are not alone. Three out of four young adults have no
real idea what they want to do or what their path in life will be when they
leave school.

*I was one of those people. I was living in a small town with only one major source
of employment, but I followed in the family tradition and joined the Navy to get
some direction in my life. I wanted to be a chef but it was a very popular choice
and I didn't have any experience so I had to choose something else…a medic. It was
good, but not what I wanted to do for the rest of my life. I made lifelong friends
among the rules and regulations and had a lot of fun. I was earning money and
surviving while I was still wondering what my path in life was.*

*I left the Navy after nine years and still had no idea on the career path I was going
to follow, so I decided to go to Europe for two years with some friends. As many
foreign travellers will tell you, when working in another country you do what you
have to, in order to survive. I had four different jobs in two years. My shortest
employment period was six weeks, the longest 12 months.*

*I want to tell you about my niece Sarah (not her real name). While at school she
was doing really well, winning academic awards, helping other students and she
had a really mature attitude for her age. Everyone said she had the potential to
achieve whatever she wanted. She left home to do a business degree at a distant
university but dropped out after a year. She moved back to her small home town
and found a job that she really liked, not only because of the industry she was in,
but also because she thrived on the responsibility and teamwork.*

*She's not earning a big income, but for her it's all about quality of life and what
makes her happy. It is a great stepping stone to the next stage of her life.*

It is not unusual for people to change their careers many times in their working life. Some people are lucky to have a passion and a path mapped out for themselves the day after leaving school, but for most of you the future is 'out of focus' and you are on a journey to find your 'place' in this world.

This is a time to work out the basic things you need to survive. The following chapter 'What to do First' tells you where you need to start.

It is also a time to start building your profile and character in this world. You will begin to get a reputation in your first job, and you want it to be a good one. Concentrate on doing your best work even if it's a boring job, and stick at it until a better opportunity comes along. This means having a professional attitude, turning up for work early, asking questions when unsure, dressing appropriately, being polite and providing great customer service. Remember, there are plenty of people out there waiting to take your job if your employer thinks somebody else can do it better than you.

AND...hopefully there are no photos floating around in cyberspace that are going to come back and 'bite you in the ass' just when you are on the verge of success.

Keep your dreams alive but follow **YOUR** dreams not anyone else's.

What To Do First

These are the things I recommend you do, to get set up for being on your own. It is mainly to do with your own and the government's paperwork. There may be government departments to assist you (if you are eligible) when times get tough.

Photocopy the following items five times:
- Birth Certificate;
- Healthcare Card;
- Passport;
- Photo ID Card;
- Driver's Licence.

Take these copies along with the original documents to a Justice of the Peace (JP) or Notary Official who can certify the copies. Their signature and stamp are official.

You will need to prove who you are to be able to register for some services and to open a bank account. You will be asked for items of proof, and depending on what they are they are usually given so many 'points' (for example; passport ? points, drivers licence ? points etc). The points have to add up to be at least some amount for your proof to be acceptable.

Use certified photocopies instead of your original documents when a number of identification points are required.

Some organisations might ask for or will accept electricity (utility) or phone accounts or bank statements as acceptable proof of who you are, provided that they have your name and address printed on them.

Check to see if your country has a Healthcare Card.
The government may provide it's citizens and residents (over a certain age), access to free or low cost medical and hospital care if they have a Healthcare Card. To find out more, go on-line and search 'Apply for a Healthcare Card.

If you have been proactive and secured employment *before* leaving school top marks to you

However if you do not have a job there are plenty of other jobs available until the right job comes along. You need to understand that you are not going to get a high paying job if you have *NO* experience. You just have to be prepared to start at the bottom like everyone else before you did, gain experience, get qualifications and work your way up to a big income.

Apply for a Tax Number (if you do not already have one)

This number stays with you for life. When you do start working you will probably need to complete tax paperwork and enter this number. If you do not have this number you will usually be taxed at a much higher rate. Go on-line and search for 'Apply for a Tax Number'

Apply for a Proof of Age card just before you turn legal age.

Your country should have an Identity Card for those people who do not have a drivers License. Pick it up as soon as possible on or after your birthday. It is a card that usually has a photo of you on it and can be used as an alternate form of ID if you do not have a driver's licence or passport. You will need to do an online search to find out how to apply for one.

If employed, you should still register at a 'welfare office'.

Get your details on file in case of future unemployment or natural disaster emergency payments. If you are unemployed you probably need to register at these centres to receive any welfare payments that you may be entitled to. There is usually a wealth of information available at the centres to help you access other services as well.

Research banks about the type of accounts they offer

You may decide to have 3 bank accounts. You will need a *DAY TO DAY ACCOUNT* which could have a debit card attached to it once you are working. This account is used for your day to day expenses. All of the money you earn from working (wages) will go into this account.

You will also need a *SAVINGS ACCOUNT* so that you can save for things like a house, car, holiday etc. Set up an automatic payment (direct debit) from your day to day account so that each time your wages go into it, 25% (or more) is automatically transferred to your savings account. Talk to your bank about how to get the best rate of interest on your money.

Open a separate *INVESTMENT ACCOUNT* for your *EMERGENCY FUND.* Set up a direct debit from your day to day account that automatically puts 10% of your wages into your emergency fund. This fund is for emergencies only and in case you are out of work for an extended period where you need to cover basic survival costs like rent, food and bills. Once you have reached a 'good' amount of money (you decide what amount) in your emergency fund you should look at investing a good portion of it for even better returns of interest.

Have a basic filing system

You are going to get a lot of paperwork from agencies like government welfare departments, superannuation companies, medical insurance companies, banks and the tax office and all this documentation needs to be filed in an organised manner for easy access. Inexpensive "expanding files" can be bought at stationery or book stores and provide separate compartments in which to keep the papers.

Scan all documentation and keep it on a USB stick

In the event of theft, fire, flood or natural disaster you will still need all official paperwork and identification such as passport, birth and qualification certificates, your CV and references, power bills, receipts for large and expensive items, bank statements, tax returns, insurance forms etc. Having those documents destroyed can delay government payments and insurance payouts.

Keep the USB stick where it is completely safe. Ask your parents or a trusted friend to hold it for you. It will need to be updated regularly. Don't keep it in your purse or wallet or anywhere where it can too easily be stolen – you might as well just hand over to the thief everything that is important to you.

Register with at least TWO employment agencies

You will need to have a Curriculum Vitae (CV). Include any references from any community or part-time work and list what your best qualities are. There are plenty of CV templates online.

Ring your employment agencies regularly

Most people sign up with an employment agency and wait for the agency to contact them. By ringing each agency Monday, Wednesday and Friday and asking them if they have any work for you, when something does come up, you are the person they will usually remember because you were not prepared to sit back and wait for a job like most other people.

Post signs for work in shop windows

Ask permission from the owner or manager first.

Go to those businesses that do the work you are looking for

Ask if there is anything available. Have a CV handy, dress smartly and be polite.

Use your right to vote

It may be a requirement to vote in local or national elections so you should enrol and be on the electoral roll once you reach the required legal age. When you vote, you select the 'party' and candidates you want to represent you in your local region, as well as the parliament, for the next term of government.

You should take the time to research; the system of government in your country, the age you have to be in order to vote and the process of how to vote.

Finding a Flat, Apartment or Room

Before applying for accommodation you need to work out where you want to live and how much you can afford to pay, not just in rent but all the other expenses such as furniture, bond or security deposit (usually one month's rent in advance), fuel/bus fares, food, electricity, mobile phone and landline, 'pay' TV, general maintenance and personal expenses such as entertainment. *REMEMBER*: When doing a budget, *UNDER ESTIMATE* your income, *OVER ESTIMATE* your expenses.

If you are finding a flat through a real estate agency or a letting agency, they will tell you all of the conditions that apply. Be warned that there may be "blacklists" shared by agencies, of the names of persons who have been bad tenants because they caused damage, were a nuisance in the neighbourhood, or failed to pay rent.

If you are finding a flat or room through a newspaper, notice in a shop, or by word of mouth, you will need to ring the contact person. The first questions over the phone may include;

- Is the room still available?
- Double checking the rent advertised,
- Is a bond payable and how much?,
- Establishing what furniture comes with the room,
- How many other housemates are there?,
- What expenses are shared?,
- Is off-street parking available?,
- What household responsibilities are there?
- What did the last electricity bill cost?

If it all sounds okay, arrange a time when you can be shown around. You will probably decide in the first 15 seconds of the visit whether you could get on with the person showing you around, and they will have done the same with you.

Unfortunately housemates are selected on first impressions but if you smile, are polite, willing to talk and can prove you can pay the rent, this goes a long way to getting the room. A viewing of the accommodation usually takes less than 10 minutes and ideally any other housemates should be there. It is important to talk with them as well.

Checks you should make

- Check for traffic noise in the bedroom if it faces the street;
- Check for locks on the bedroom door, and who has keys.. Keep in mind previous tenants may well still have keys in their possession;
- Point out any unsatisfactory conditions issues in the room, such as exposed wiring, loose power and light switches, flaking paint or carpet stains and ask whether and when they will be repaired.

Other questions to ask about how the 'flat' operates

- Do you have to buy your own food?
- What space has been set aside for you to store your food?
- Is there a payment required for communal groceries?
- Who owns the property?
- Who do I pay rent to? Is cash okay or do I need to set up a direct debit from my bank?
- Confirm the 'bond' amount. Can you pay it off? Make sure you get a receipt when you pay the bond.
- What other storage space is there?
- If someone moves out how is the rent covered till someone moves in?
- Is there a rat, cockroach, termite, snake or flood problem?
- Is the house a party house?
- Are the neighbours noisy?

NOTE: A room without furniture always looks small. For peace of mind you can take a tape measure to confirm that your furniture will fit. Take photos of any damage in the room before you move in and ask the person renting the room if it can be fixed. If it can't and you still decide to move in, your photos can be used to show you haven't damaged the place further when you leave and it gives you a reason to ask for your bond back in full.

If you want to move into a vacant flat, apartment or house
You will need to first view the inside of the house/flat/apartment. The renting agent or landlord should be present and you should make note of the things that need attention. This will be anything that is in bad condition as well as possible safety issues, condition of walls, furniture, carpets etc.

Switch on taps, lights, the oven, fans, air conditioners etc to make sure they all work. If you are keen on the place, fill in an application and ask the agent to get the noted problems sorted out before you move in. Looking at your application the agent will want to satisfy themselves you have a good character and will ask for any previous renting references. Once you have been approved ask the agent when any major repairs are likely to be completed so you can pay the bond and start moving in.

Before you and the housemates sign the rental agreement
Read it thoroughly and look to see if anything is unclear. Ask questions. What is the rental period? Can it be renewed? When is the rent due to increase?

Bond (also known as a Security Deposit)
You will probably be charged a 'bond' of approximately one (1) month's rent. This money is kept for the owner of the property in case there is unpaid rent or damage to the property. You will be given this money back if you honour your rental agreement and there was no damage to the property while you were living there. You will need to find out who actually keeps your bond and the process of claiming it back. Make sure you keep the receipt and take photos of any previous damage so you can compare them to the condition of the property when you move out.

The entry inspection paperwork (inventory) will need to be completed and handed back to the agent usually within a few days. It details any minor problems and previous damage you find with the accommodation that you need the agent to sort out.

It is essential you fill the Inventory in as fully as possible – every crack, mark, stain, obvious and even not-so-obvious damage. If you don't record these issues at the beginning, you could be charged to have them all fixed when you move out.

Once the 'bond' has been paid

Any major repairs should have been completed. Keep the bond receipt safe. You will be given the keys and be allowed to move in. Each housemate should get their own set of keys.

You should get your 'bond' money back if you keep the place undamaged, clean and tidy

When you move out of the property, an inspection is done by the agent or owner and anything that has been damaged *outside* of normal use (wear and tear), is taken off the amount of 'bond' you get back. Once an amount of 'bond' (to be refunded) is agreed, the agent or owner should arrange for that amount to be paid to you. You should double-check the actual process.

Get all the house mates together to establish some ground rules

Do house mates want a phone (landline), 'Pay TV' (what channels?), who looks after the lawns and puts out the rubbish and recycling bins, where does everyone park their vehicle, whose name is going on the electricity bill?

Collecting the rent

Usually it will be done by the person who has their name on the rental agreement. Whenever you hand over any money for rent and bills you should ask for a receipt. This keeps track of not only your expenses, but can be used when there are disputes regarding payment.

Set up a suitable calendar and mark down important dates (rent, monthly bills)

This idea lets everyone in the flat know when bills are due so that they can budget for them.

You should expect occasional Inspections

During the time you rent a place, there may be a requirement that it is occasionally inspected for the owner. This is to make sure the place is not being damaged but also to fix any problems you may have. A letter will usually be sent out by the agent or owner letting the tenants know that an inspection is coming up. If no-one is going to be home the agent/owner will have a set of keys to gain entry. With the letter there may be paperwork for you to write down any problems that need fixing and you need to organise the people living there to make sure the place is clean and tidy and there is access to the bedrooms.

Being clean and tidy

This is the one of the main things you need to be concerned about. Everyone sharing the living space has their own life and *NO-ONE* wants to, or has the time to be picking up someone else's stuff or cleaning up someone else's mess. Being told once to tidy up your mess you are forgiven. Being told three times or more and you will make enemies.

Neighbours

Get to know your neighbours. Many people don't do this because they are too busy with their own lives, yet neighbours can be a lifeline in an emergency and look after your 'place' when you are on holiday. They are also likely to be more forgiving when you make a little extra noise.

If your 'place' has been sold

You should have been given plenty of notice (usually at least three weeks but it may be different in your area) that you need to move out. Once everyone has moved out their belongings, you need to do an *exit* inspection and use the *entry* inspection paperwork (that you kept) as a guide to what has changed. Is it 'wear and tear' or is it actual damages you will have to pay for?

If you want your 'bond' refunded

You should give the whole inside of the place a good clean. You should look at your rental agreement to see what your requirements are when moving out of the property (carpet cleaning, pest report etc). You may need to present receipts to the agent/owner as evidence of cleaning being done, along with the keys for the premises, in order to receive your 'bond' back.

Once you have handed the keys back to the agent

They will do their own exit inspection. Ask if you can be present during their inspection. Have any previous photos (from when you moved in) ready to compare with the current condition. You should ring them the day following the inspection to see how their inspection went (if you were not there) and to ask how much of the 'bond' they are authorising to be released.

NOTE: Before you receive the bond or security deposit from your previous place you will usually have been required to pay another bond on your new place. In some circumstances (a government agency) it may be possible to have your bond transferred.

32

Medical emergency information

In an emergency medical situation, there is limited work the ambulance staff can do if they do not know your medical history. They need to know what medications you are taking, any medical conditions you suffer from, and any allergies you have to medications. You may want to write all this down, put it in an envelope and write on it your nominated emergency person and number to contact. Tell your housemates where you keep the envelope so they can access it in case of emergency. It could save your life.

Buying a Car

The problem many teenagers make when buying a car

Guys, especially, buy a car to impress their friends and the opposite sex, not for practical purposes and then find they have a high level of debt. For example; they might buy a $30 000 car. By the time they pay it off in, say, 5 years it will have cost them about $44 000 in loan repayments but it will only be worth about $15 000 when they sell it. Sure they have a nice car for five years, but chances are those loan repayments will affect their ability to save money and enjoy life and they will probably lose $29 000. Losing that amount of money is not the way to 'get ahead in life'. Upgrade your car only when you can *afford* to do so. A good clean reliable car can be bought for a fraction of the above cost and still get you and your friends where you need to go, which is all you need to get started.

How to Purchase a Vehicle.

A Car Dealer. Check government web sites in your country about the laws car dealers must follow when selling cars. You should take special note of any warranty they are legally required to offer. A 'warranty' is similar to a guarantee whereby for a certain period, if you have problems with the vehicle you bought, you can return the vehicle, get a refund or get the problem repaired. Ideally you should have saved all of the money to buy the vehicle because many car loans usually have a higher rate of interest attached.

A Private Seller. These are people who have advertised their vehicle through a newspaper, the internet or on the side of the road. There is more risk when buying from a private seller. There is *NO* warranty available so you need to have the vehicle thoroughly checked out by a mechanic, testing station or someone else who knows a lot about buying a vehicle. Provided the right questions are asked and you have done some research done on the cars history and it's current condition, buying from a private seller can be a good experience.

Choose the type of vehicle you *NEED* not *WANT*

Think carefully about the vehicle you need (2 door, 4 door, station wagon or estate, 4 wheel drive.). As a general rule, the smaller the vehicle you buy, the less it will cost you to run it. Insurance, filling the petrol tank and maintenance costs can be a lot more expensive for larger cars.

You will need to work out how much you are willing to spend.

Not only the actual purchase price of the vehicle but other costs such as insurance, registration, an inspection certificate to state the vehicle is in a 'road worthy' condition, associated costs to bring the vehicle up to standard, running costs (fuel, oil) as well as looking after (maintaining) it.

Visit your country's 'cars guide' website

These sites contain a very good list of actions, questions and thought processes you should go through to have successful trouble-free car buying.

Take someone who knows about cars with you, to look at one.

Lift the hood (bonnet) and get the owner to start the engine. A *cold engine start* is needed because a warm engine will hide sounds like the engine running roughly that may indicate an engine problem. A warm engine also has 'clear exhaust' smoke whereas a cold engine may blow different coloured smoke out of the exhaust which can indicate various problems. Go on-line and search for 'different colour exhaust smoke' to find out more.

While you are looking at the engine find the Vehicle Identification Number (VIN) number on the maker's plate and *NOTE IT DOWN*. You will need to get it checked.

If all seems well with the engine, take the car for a drive. Do all the lights, turn signals, mirrors, wipers and seatbelts work? Find a quiet street and test the steering by gently weaving the car from side to side to test if the steering rack seems solid and to see whether the shock absorbers make a 'clunking' sound. You should also drive the vehicle in a full circle to see if there are any problems.

Check the speedometer kilometres (or miles) against the condition of the car. Look for signs it has been in an accident. If everything appears ok and you are still interested tell the owner you will call them the next day. This gives you time to do some research on the price of the car regarding its year, make, model and condition as well as checking out the VIN number (see next page).

Rust

Open the boot and look under the bottom liner, at the spare wheel area. Look for holes and evidence of rust. Also check the joins where the roof and doors meet. Look for bubbling paint all around the car. It indicates rust.

If the vehicle does not have a current 'road worthy' Certificate

Do not accept the owner saying it will only need minor repairs to pass. If you are very interested tell the seller, but suggest you go halves in the cost for an inspection certificate. Arrange a time to meet at the vehicle inspection centre, view the report and negotiate price regarding the vehicles defects if you are still interested. If not, the money you spent has stopped you from making a big mistake and it's time to look elsewhere.

Check the VIN number of any car you are thinking of buying

In your country look on the government, State or Provincial database where your car is registered (there may be a small fee) to see whether the vehicle has been stolen, written off or there is an outstanding loan attached to it. If it has, *DO NOT BUY IT!!*

In some countries you need to get your vehicle inspected regularly

You can improve your pass rate at a vehicle inspection and testing facility by doing some basic checks at home; the horn, lights, indicators, handbrake, number plate light, windscreen washers and wipers and tyre tread depth including the spare tyre. Check also for rust around the structural supports.

Make sure your car is tidy. A messy car indicates a 'sloppy' attitude and the vehicle tester may make more detailed checks.

Remove all valuables

Before lending, storing or dropping off your car to get fixed or inspected remove anything of value as it may go missing. This includes toolboxes, spare cash, documents in the glove compartment, etc.

Driving Information

Get a parent or adult to show you basic car maintenance
It is usually the law that your car is always required to be in a 'road worthy' condition. To keep it that way and to keep your car working properly there are checks such as tyre condition, wiper blades, all lights and light covers that need to be done regularly. Under the hood (bonnet) you need to check fluid levels (oil, water and brake fluid) as well as the condition of fan belts and cooling hoses. You also need to know how to change a flat tyre (puncture) safely. If you live in a cold climate don't forget to add antifreeze to the radiator. Remember that at a roadside breath test, if the police suspect your car is not in a road worthy condition they may stop you from driving it.

Did you know that your insurance company may not 'pay out' for any accident damage if your car has not been properly looked after?
That means lack of tread depth on the tyres, faulty lights and turning signals (indicators), rust issues or lack of a vehicle inspection certificate or registration etc. This will also include whether you were under the influence of drugs/ alcohol at the time of the accident. Check your insurance policy for further information.

Before you get in your car to drive
Take a walk around the car and see if you have a tyre that is down on pressure and to see if there are any other issues like broken lights, fluid leaks etc.

Get a 'hands free' mobile kit for your car
Reaching for a mobile phone is one of the big causes of driver distraction. You either need to get a hands free phone kit or to pull over on the side of the

road and have your phone conversation there. There may be severe penalties for talking on your phone while driving.

Tie down loose items on the back seats
Braking hard to avoid unexpected hazards and being involved in an accident can make the simplest objects become dangerous 'missiles'.

Any nervousness or hesitation can lead to an accident

When on the road you need to think about what you are *doing* and what you are *going to do*. Make clear decisions and act accordingly.

Look 100 metres ahead of you, NOT 20 metres

By constantly scanning the road from your vehicle to 100 metres ahead allows you to judge any potential problems that might occur and to act accordingly. These problems could be animals straying onto the road, pedestrians, cyclists, farm vehicles coming out of driveways, children playing on the side of the road etc.

When following a car, use the three second rule

When you follow too closely to a vehicle, you do not have enough time to react if the car in front brakes or swerves suddenly. The three second rule (on roads that are in good condition and in clear weather) is used to give you enough time.

> *How to work it out:* Pick something ahead like a road sign. When the car in front passes that point, say to yourself aloud "One thousand two thousand three thousand". If *your* car has passed that same point before you finish saying that, then you are following too close.

On roads that are wet, 'greasy' and in bad weather it is best to double or even triple the three second rule to give you plenty of time to stop if necessary.

A driver's lack of attention probably causes more deaths on the road than the 'fatal 4' (speed, seatbelts, alcohol, fatigue) put together

If you are driving on the open road you need to be paying attention to what is happening in front of and around your vehicle. You should be looking at the road ahead, judging the distance to vehicles in front of you and braking when necessary as well as quickly searching in your mirrors for potential problems. It is when you are suddenly distracted by something that problems start occurring.

Even when you are driving slowly bad things can happen quickly, because you probably believed you had enough time to change the music, adjust the radio, do your make-up, talk on your phone, eat, have a drink, argue with your partner, drop your cigarette and get distracted by children or pets. Obviously this becomes dangerous because it takes your attention away from what is happening on the road ahead of you.

Be aware of your vehicle's 'Blind Spot'

Down each side of your vehicle there is an area *BETWEEN* what you can see with your rear vision mirror and your vehicle's side mirror called the 'blind spot'. A whole vehicle, but especially a motor cycle, can be hidden there. Before you change lanes you *NEED* to quickly turn your head to check this area and then use your turning signal to change lanes.

Be aware of your vehicle being in another vehicle's 'Blind Spot'

There are occasions when you are on a multi lane road and a car is just in front of you in another lane. You should take action to get out of their blind spot.

Operate your turning signal BEFORE you apply the brakes

When the driver behind you sees you brake for no apparent reason it can make them angry. Angry drivers are dangerous drivers. Please signal at least 3 seconds before you need to brake when wanting to make a turn

Watch out for cyclists

When driving any vehicle and passing a cyclist you should leave a minimum of 1 metre clear when passing cyclists in a 60km/h or less speed zone and 1.5 metres where the speed limit is over 60km/h.

Speed is a factor in only around 5% of road deaths

This will be shocking news to most people. But the simple reason is… when you drive fast, you are concentrating on the road. In 30 years of driving I have never (or seen anyone else) take their eyes off the road when overtaking a car (you have to speed to do this) because they have to judge the distance if a car comes the other way. It is when you think you have time to do things (usually driving slower) that you are easily distracted.

Speed does become a danger when you are driving too fast
- for the conditions of the road (ice, snow, rain, drizzle);
- for the capabilities of your vehicle;
- for your own skill level;
- and you are distracted.

Make sure you have a 'charged' mobile phone when driving.

This is especially important for long trips. Having a charged mobile phone can be the difference between life and death if you witness or are involved in an accident. The exact location of any emergency on the road is very important.

If you are the first person at the scene of an accident, call the emergency number in your country and know your *EXACT* location.

A fire extinguisher and first aid kit can save lives

Having these in your car at all times and knowing how to use them can save peoples lives.

Yes there are 'idiots' out on the road EVERY day

Do not get angry and do anything that puts you or them in danger. If their driving was really bad, take a note of their registration number and report it to the police. Do not follow them because you do not know what you could be getting into.

Parking

When parking it is a good idea to reverse into a space (you will need good reversing skills to do this). This makes it easier for you to check oncoming traffic before you pull into the traffic lane. It also has the benefit of being able to drive straight out if a situation comes up where you need to exit the area quickly.

Hitch-hiking

I do not recommend you do it but for tips and safety recommendations go online and search 'hitchwiki'.

To fully understand the road rules in your Country, State or Province, get a copy of the 'learning to drive' book from your local Department of Transport or Automobile Association

Insurance

Insurance is used to protect your lifestyle if something happens such as an accident, fire, theft or natural disaster and you suffer a large loss.

Insurance is offered by companies on your health, income, your life, your partners and/or your children's lives, funeral, your car and contents of your home. The insurance companies will pay out a certain amount depending on your policy details, if you suffer a loss, or the loss of the use of, the above mentioned things.

When you are young, chances are you don't have many things of high value that you need to insure. However your car and your income should be insured as you could lose a lot of money if you have a car accident or you are injured and can't work. As you get older and have more things of value, you need to work out the things in your life that need insuring.

A payment for insurance protection is called a 'premium'. To have insurance protection you need to talk to an insurance company about what you want to insure. There are many insurance companies to choose from and it may be a good idea for you to go to an 'insurance broker'.

An insurance broker compares the policies from different insurance companies and finds the best policy to suit your needs. Look in the yellow pages for one in your area.

You always need to remember to ask questions, read and fully understand all paperwork (documents), compare prices and information from other insurance companies (research), get some good advice from an adult role model and then if there are no concerns, fill in an application.

The first rule is *LOCK IT* or *LOSE IT*
If it's worth insuring it's worth making sure it's safe. You can reduce the heartache from theft if you securely lock your room or flat when you go out, and when you are asleep. And always lock your car if you are not using it.

Read and understand any insurance paperwork you are sent

This is very important. You will have signed on for insurance and you are being sent all the details you and the insurance company talked about. You need to check it thoroughly and contact them if something is not right.

Risk

For insurance companies it is all about **RISK**. The higher the risks are to them from you making a claim, the higher your monthly premiums will be. The risks they take into account are your age, your experience, your lifestyle, where you live, the type of job you have, the type of car you drive etc.

So if you are 18, drive a high powered sports car and list base jumping as a hobby you are probably going to have very, very high insurance premiums or will be refused insurance, because the insurance company will believe the risk of having to 'pay out' for you is very high.

However as you get older and your driving experience grows, you should build up a good driving history. If you also live in a 'safe' neighbourhood, your car is kept in an area off the street or in a garage and you don't use it much, then you most likely will be accepted for insurance because you are viewed as 'low risk' (of making a claim) and as such, your insurance premiums should be much less.

What is an 'Excess'?

You need to understand what an 'Excess' is. On any claim that is payable by the insurance company, you will have to pay what is called an 'excess'. It's what you have to pay as your share of the cost of replacing the insured item.

The lower you make your 'excess' the higher your monthly payments (premium) will be. Say you suffer a theft of an item that costs $1 000 and your excess is $500. Because that excess is a part of your insurance policy when making a claim, if the insurance company agrees to pay your claim, they will subtract the 'excess' off the amount you are claiming ($1 000) and give you just $500. This is why insurance is better for expensive things because the 'excess' is a small fraction of the value of the thing the insurance company is paying you for.

It is not worth claiming for insurance if the quoted repair costs are less than the 'excess' nominated in your policy. A broken window on your car from someone breaking in might cost you $300, but if your 'excess' on your insurance policy is $500, then there obviously is no use claiming insurance.

Review your insurance policies

If you do get any insurance you should review the policy(s) every 6 months and if you need to adjust it for any changes that have occurred, then ring and talk to your insurance company. You also need to thoroughly read any insurance documents and make sure you understand what is required from you. Some policies include conditions that if you don't do what they say, such as keeping your car locked, or in roadworthy condition, then you won't be able to make an insurance claim if it gets stolen or damaged.

Record your insured items

You need to take photos of large or expensive things you have bought and have insured. Keep all paperwork and scan them onto a separate USB stick. That USB needs to be away from your home because if your home is burgled or destroyed, how do you prove that you owned these things to now make a claim?

Filing an insurance claim

Contact your insurance company if you need to make a claim. Forms can usually be downloaded from their website. Insurance companies very easily refuse to pay out on items when their paperwork is not completed properly or you have not provided enough evidence in your claim.

Your Legal Requirement

When filling in paperwork for an insurance claim, you are *legally required* to fill in the forms *TRUTHFULLY*. There are big penalties for entering false information.

Premium rises

Despite what insurance companies may claim, your annual insurance premium will almost always rise if you make a claim. This is because you are now seen as a 'higher' risk to them of making future claims.

Even if you haven't made a claim but it has been a bad financial year for the insurance company they may still raise your premium. You should contact them and ask them "Why you should be penalised?" If you are unhappy with the result, contact other insurance companies to find a better value price.

Identity Theft

If your personal details are stolen you can lose *EVERYTHING*.

What is Identity Crime?

> **Identity** means the name of a person who is living or has died.
> **Identity Fabrication** is described as inventing a completely new person.
> **Identity Manipulation** is described as changing your own identity.
> **Identity Theft** refers to the stealing of someone else's identity.
> **Identity Crime** or **Identity Fraud** is a term used to cover the above instances where the purpose has been to commit a crime.

Take time to think how often each day you are required to use anything that tells others who you are. Your personal information helps you open bank accounts, go shopping, order things online, fill your vehicle with petrol, get money out of an ATM, register for courses, apply for credit, apply for government benefits, apply for a passport, apply for a job and get a drivers licence etc.

What does a criminal do with *YOUR* information?
If you *DO NOT* protect your personal details, someone can steal those details and use them to become *YOU* and buy things they need with *YOUR* money. As you get older and have more money, the task for a person wanting to steal your details becomes easier especially as your life becomes busy and you are more care-free about it happening to you. *DO NOT* fall into this trap.

If someone steals your identity and builds up expenses, loans and debts in your name, your credit rating may be severely affected and you will not be eligible for any loans in the future. It will take a long time and it will be a very difficult process to prove your innocence and regain your credibility.

How easy would it be for someone to access your mail? Bank statements and credit cards are sent in the mail followed by your *PIN* number a few days later. All a criminal needs is basic information to get to the next step of stealing your identity.

What can you do to protect yourself?

- Get yourself a Post Office Box or at the very least a lock for your letterbox and clear your mail often;
- Reduce the amount of mail you get by registering online with trusted organisations that should have secure websites (banks and government departments etc), in order to apply for benefit payments, view account statements or make payments;
- As soon as you lose a credit card report it to the bank that issued it. That way you limit your responsibility for anything bought on it;
- Be careful what you do with your rubbish, especially receipts that have your personal details on them. Shred them or burn them (carefully);
- Documents with your personal information you wish to store should be kept in a secure place at your parent's home, especially if you are in a rented house with others;
- Shield your PIN number when entering it onto keypads at ATM or EFTPOS terminals and be aware of your surroundings. Are people too close or acting suspiciously?
- Make sure your computer and mobile phone devices have up-to-date and current virus and security software;
- Do not make any payments or do bank statement checks on public computers like internet cafes, or unsecured wireless hotspots;
- Be very careful who you provide your personal details to and the reason they need your details. Ask them "Is there a third party that receives those details?," and stress that you do not give permission for your personal information to be passed on;
- You *NEED* to look at bank statements to see if anything unusual has occurred like payments and large amounts have been taken out. Double check at the bank as there is usually a reference code associated with a payment;
- Use only trusted online payment websites for items won at online auctions or purchased online. Never make payments outside of trusted systems—particularly for goods which you have not yet received;
- Credit and Debit cards with microchips are more secure than cards with magnetic strips;
- Beware of scams promising huge payments from overseas countries (people, lotteries, banks), if you supply your personal information such as bank details. *DO NOT* respond to their emails or letters;

- If you are unsure about anything, try and do some follow up research. Is there a contact number? Listen for any foreign accent and remember they are trained to trick you;
- With social networking sites you never know who you are actually 'talking' to. Use the most secure settings on your device and beware of giving away personal information. There is a danger when accepting unwanted 'friend' requests;

For more information go on-line and search for 'Identity Crime'.

If you think you are the victim of Identity Fraud contact the Police.

NOTE: I had someone ring me up and say that they had won $40 million dollars in a US lottery and they had chosen me to receive $10000 dollars and could they have my bank account details. It was 3am in the morning and I took down their name and asked them to ring back the next day. In the meantime I went online and checked the name and sure enough the white middle class American name checked out as a lottery winner. The problem though, was that the person ringing me had an Indian accent. So I had great fun asking him to explain that fact when he called the next night.

Your Mobile Phone

As well as being a device for entertainment, knowledge and communication your phone is very important in an emergency (for you or someone else). For that reason alone, you need to make sure your mobile phone has *ENOUGH* 'charge' in the batteries to make a call to save your or someone else's life. You also need to know *YOUR EXACT LOCATION* so that the emergency services can get to where you are.

Use your mobile phone sensibly
Using a mobile phone can be dangerous because it takes your attention away from what is happening around you. Using headphones is even more dangerous because they block out your body's natural instinct to warn you of danger. Using your mobile phone when sitting down is usually safer than walking around.

Use your mobile phone *ONLY* when you are away from people
It may be considered rude to use it when people are in a group.

When was the last time you cleaned your phone
Mobile phones have been shown to be wonderful homes for bacteria. Clean and disinfect it twice a week; you can get suitable tissues from your drug store (chemist).

Know that photos and 'sexts' you have sent can go *ANYWHERE*.
A picture lives forever…*FOREVER.* You have no control over who views any naked or revealing pictures of yourself or 'sexts' that you send out, and where they end up. People you meet who have seen them may form the wrong opinion of you and it could cost you the career or opportunity you wanted.

Before your mobile phone is stolen
In most countries your phone has an IMEI number If your phone is stolen your network provider can block the phone from being used if you tell them the phones IMEI number. Dial *#06# (star, hash, zero, six, hash) now and write down the number that comes up on your screen and keep it handy.

Storing your medical information in your phone

If you are 'blacked out' (unconscious), emergency personnel need to know certain information about you in order to start saving your life. If they do not know this information, they are limited to doing basic life support until you arrive at hospital which may be a long way away. However, if they know about your allergies, any medications you are taking and any medical conditions you have, they can give you more effective treatment that may give you a better chance of survival.

You always have your phone with you so why not make it a tool that may save your life. In your phone book make a new contact *000 Medical Info* (this will be easily visible on the first page of your contacts) and write down your medical conditions, allergies and any medication you are taking.

If you are going out somewhere with friends, tell one or two of them what your phone access code is, if an emergency arises. You probably should show them where in your phone the information is stored, so they can tell the emergency staff. You can do the same for them.

Your phone is prone to viruses just like a computer

'Opening' anything can lead you to have an infected phone. Think 'Do I really need to access this?' Have an anti-malware app and update it regularly. Only click on links if you are expecting them.

To change your mobile SIM card

Can't find your special key to unlock the SIM compartment on your mobile phone? If the access port is a tiny hole, open out a paper clip and use the end to trigger the release mechanism.

How to get 'quick' human assistance in a menu of options

A few ways to get past a long line of options may be to press the '0' button repeatedly, not speak clearly and to use certain swear words. For further information go online and search for 'ways to talk to a human when calling a business'.

Tips for Around the House

If you are living at home, not only do you need to start becoming more responsible but you should be making your parents' life a lot easier by helping them out. You can do this by learning to cook, clean and do the laundry etc. It is these skills you are going to need when you move away from home and start sharing a flat or apartment. Not only will your room mates be happy but the opposite sex will be as well, especially if you clean up after you finish making a mess.

Always wash your hands before handling food
Things you don't think about, like your mobile phone and money are really bad for containing bacteria. When was the last time you disinfected your mobile phone? Do it a couple of times a week.

Clean up after yourself
If you are an untidy person be untidy in your own room. Being messy in a shared living space will not be tolerated for long. Put it this way, how would you feel always picking up or cleaning up other people's mess.

Food poisoning
Can happen even in the most modern countries. Cook all meat well, store food properly and check the 'use by' date of food. When eating out, the most common restaurant foods that can give you food poisoning are meat, seafood and prepared salads, especially cream-based ones such as coleslaw and potato salad.

Plan your meals for the week
Doing this will help your budget. You will know what ingredients to put on your shopping list. There are many recipes for meals that use only four ingredients and can be completed in 20 minutes or less. Make up more than you need and freeze the rest for future meals when you don't feel like cooking. This also cuts down on wanting to get 'fast food' because you already have something in the freezer and it *only* needs reheating.

Keep your takeaway containers, they are handy for leftovers to go into the fridge, and they stack better than round plastic containers.

Make a shopping list to cut down on 'impulse buying'

Buy only what you need and reward yourself one small treat. Not having a shopping list means you buy what you want, not what you need and those unnecessary things may add 30% to your shopping bill.

Eat before you go grocery shopping

Shopping on an empty stomach means you are a victim to all the smells in the supermarket but especially those coming out of the bakery and it is not going to help your waistline or your budget.

Buy in bulk where possible.

Good savings are made on high use items like sugar, cereals etc. Make sure you have enough containers to store the extra products.

'Home brands' are fine.

These products have the store's own brand and are usually made at the same factories as the branded products, but they are in plainer packaging and cost a lot less.

Bag loose fruit and vegetables yourself.

When food is packed into containers it can be a lot more expensive because the store has to pay someone to do it. With loose items like fruit and vegetables pack your own and save money.

Wash all raw fruit and vegetables under water before use.

This should get rid of the chemicals that linger after the growing, processing and storing of the items.

Learn to cook.

Not only does it help your self sufficiency but it will impress the opposite sex. Have a couple of 'signature' dishes. These are meals you are good at making (spaghetti bolognaise, a roast meal etc). Noodles on rice is *NOT* an option.

When cooking to impress.

A chef friend of mine suggests that when you are cooking to impress people, whether or not you need it, always fry up an onion. The smell gives the impression that you are really talented in the kitchen. Therefore keep people out of the kitchen or you will be 'busted'.

Wherever possible, pack your lunch for work or uni.
It is cheaper than buying your lunch. You can save $2 000/year.

Carpet stain remover
Immediately pour some soda water, lemonade or ginger ale to cover the stain. The chemical reaction of the 'fizz' will lift the stain. Dab frequently with paper towels to remove.

Preserve fresh flowers
The water that flowers are in becomes brown because of bacteria. To delay the bacteria growth, use a couple of teaspoons of either dish washing liquid, detergent or disinfectant and add it to the fresh water. Repeat every two – three days.

To unblock a drain
If a plunger does not work, sprinkle a cup of baking soda in the drain followed by a cup of vinegar. Leave for a few minutes. The resulting chemical reaction will hopefully dissolve enough of the material and then you can flush the system with warm water.

Refreshing the inside of a fridge
Wipe interior with a mixture of 2 cups warm water and 2 teaspoons of vanilla essence. Then put a small open container of baking soda on a shelf and leave overnight to absorb any lingering smells.

Remove odours from wooden chopping boards
Wipe down with a cloth dampened with white vinegar.

Reduce the 'crying' from onions
Peel the onion and run under cold water for about 10 seconds. The water reduces the amount of irritant onions let off when you chop them up.

Read all instruction manuals carefully
In order to use items correctly, to maintain warranties, and avoid injury, take the time to read the product manuals (not all washing machines work the same way).

To limit ironing

Fold or hang washing straight off the clothes line.

Keep a first aid kit in your house and car

First aid kits of all sizes are usually available at large chemists and drug stores. You should get one for your household and one for your car. They need to include band-aids, gloves, sanitiser, triangular and crepe bandages, antiseptic cream and lotion, tape etc. A first aid course will teach you how to use these items for basic accidents.

When visiting someone else's place

As a polite and courteous gesture, make it a habit of taking something along; a bottle of wine, meat for the BBQ, fruit pack or something small for any children.

Throwing Your Own Party

Put a 'ping pong, ball in the toilet bowl so that the guys have something to aim at and your toilet floor won't be as messy the next day.

Got your attention and a smile? Good, but now it gets a bit more serious.

For you as the host, the main focus of the party, whatever the occasion, is all about *THE SAFETY* of the people you invite and secondly that there is no damage to your or your housemate's stuff. Put valuables away and lock the door to rooms you don't want people going into. If the door can't be locked, put a notice on it "Private – Keep Out!"

YOU could be legally held responsible if there is damage caused to another person or property, by someone at your party who is drunk and/or violent. For this reason alone you should restrict the amount of alcohol *YOU* drink.

Your friends of the same age will have limited experience about how alcohol affects them so you need to make your venue as safe as possible for them. Your friends should make their own arrangements to get home safely. You should have a taxi number in your phone as a back up and maybe pre-book some taxis for after midnight.

Contact your local police or look at their website as you may be able to register your party before the event. If a web site is available it should provide you with all the information you need for a successful and safe party.

It is against the law to supply alcohol to anyone under a certain age. Check your local laws at the police station or their web site.

When enough alcohol enters the equation, it may change a person's personality to the point where they say and do stuff that they wouldn't normally do.

With some people they get tired and sit somewhere quietly, other people talk a lot, some people get a bit 'flirty', others become the life of the party and then there are those who turn into really funny people, complete idiots or get aggressive and want to fight everyone. You need to understand that you **CANNOT REASON WITH A PERSON WHO IS DRUNK**. The options are to call their parents or a sober friend to come and pick them up, or if they start getting violent, the police.

If you are having your own party, you can control who attends by inviting people yourself through calling or texting them and saying whether they can bring a partner. The only people that may send out written invitations are girls because guys simply don't do it. Your invitation should include the time to attend, and what to bring in the way of food or drink.

However if it is a flat/house/apartment party, it could be a little harder to control who comes along. The best way around possible 'gatecrashers' is to talk to your house mates and agree to send out texts and calls personally and not to advertise it on social media.

Out of courtesy you should inform your neighbours about five or so days before the event so they can make arrangements to be away, come over and join you or keep pets inside.

HINTS FOR A BETTER PARTY

- Look around the property for hazards that could cause injury to people not only when they are drunk. Limit the danger to people by thinking about things like swimming pools, gas heaters, portable cookers, mats, small stuff lying around (clutter) etc;
- Have good lighting;
- Have the party in the most private part of the property which is usually at the back;
- Have only one entry and exit point to the party area so that you can restrict any unwelcome people.
- Serve food and have a lot of it. It delays the effects of alcohol. You supply the snacks, bread and salads and get guests to bring their own meat for cooking. Make available plenty of non alcoholic drinks.

- Do not allow people to drink or smoke at the front of the property as it encourages other people to join in, as well as complaints from neighbours.
- Have plenty of toilet paper *IN* the toilet area.
- Keep the noise level down especially after midnight (it's the law). The music volume should go down a few levels at about 11.30pm and be turned off at midnight.
- Only *TIME* will sober up a person, not food, not water, not making them sick (they could choke), not activity, not a cold shower. You *WILL* need to call for an ambulance on the emergency number for anyone who is 'blacked out' (unconscious).
- Learn about the First-Aid *RECOVERY POSITION*. This is a position to use for a person who is breathing but is unconscious. It is not difficult to do and may save that person's life. Go on-line and search for 'Recovery Position'. One of the many sites will show you how to do it.

PLEASE NOTE: *An unconscious (blacked out) person who stays on their back can die, because their tongue relaxes, falls to the back of their throat and blocks their airway so they can't breathe.*

Study

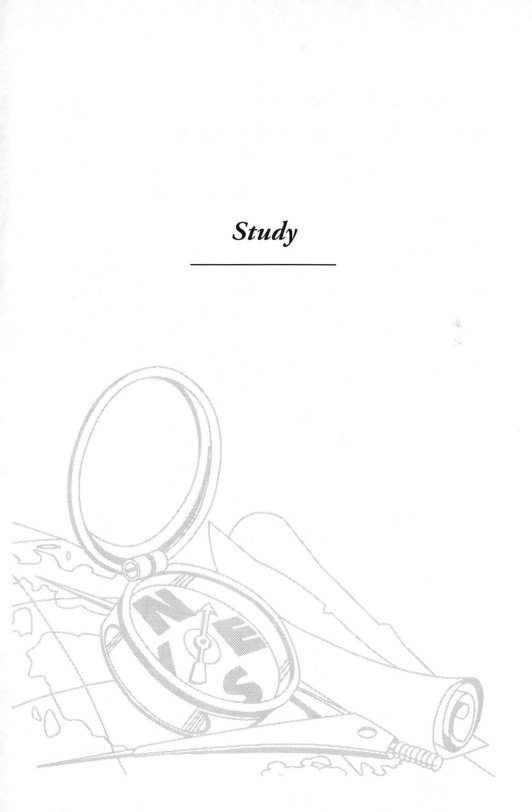

Going to University

You will need to choose the *RIGHT* University

The right university contains the courses you want to do. Know exactly what those courses and subjects are, go online and search the websites of universities that have those courses available. You can usually make an entry application to those universities online.

Be aware of specific course and subject requirements

You need to know the requirements of each subject to be completed and in which order during the term of your course. Certain subjects must be passed before doing future subjects later in the degree. Again, plan your whole course at the start to save yourself time and worry.

There may also be pre-requisite courses for future courses (eg a qualification in Business Administration in order to complete a course in Justice Administration).

Talk to the faculty advisor

Find out what courses you need to do based on your goals and how to register for them. Especially make certain your subject choices have the correct amount of accreditation points needed to meet the requirements of your qualification. Be aware not all subjects are available every semester – **you will need to plan the whole course in advance.**

Read *ALL* the university documents that you are sent

This is especially relevant to what the university and accommodation does or doesn't provide. Note down any contact names and phone numbers. Keep all the university paperwork in a safe place.

Make sure you understand every aspect of *ANY* agreement *BEFORE* you sign it

This is a very important thing you should always do anyway. Any university paperwork that requires your signature means you will make a legal commitment to something and you need to fully understand what that is, *BEFORE* you sign it.

Get your payments sorted out early

Obtain from the university the exact breakdown of fees you must pay. If you are on a scholarship or sponsorship or have a Student Loan agreement, know the difference you must pay. Get payments and deposits sorted out early to avoid the frustration of long queues. Keep receipts organized and in an easy-to-access location because you never know when there might be a time where proof of payment is demanded.

Make a list of what to take

You should take all university paperwork that has been sent to you (in an organised file), as well as bank statements, credit/debit cards, spare passport photos, accommodation provisions, USB sticks, sports equipment and a range of suitable clothing.

Get familiar with the surroundings

The sooner you feel comfortable in your new environment, the better. Walk around with other people and explore your accommodation and campus. Know where you need to be and at what time. Make your room as comfortable and as welcoming as possible. You will be spending a lot of time there.

Be aware of the university calendar of events

Keep your own calendar or diary to note down the events that are important to you.

BUDGET your Money

You have to live within the amount of money allocated to you. See the section in this book on budgeting. If you can afford the time to get a part time job once you are used to your schedule, that will help relieve some pressure but if it starts to affect your amount of quality sleep or exam results you will need to cut back the working hours.

Take time to settle in

It will take longer than you think to meet new friends and feel comfortable around them, as well as accommodation rituals and your day to day routine. Allow yourself three months to settle in.

Get used to living communally

Be a model housemate. Clean up after yourself (use disinfectant occasionally). Wash yourself daily and use deodorant to smell good. Keep the noise down (voice, music) as people are sleeping and studying. One time you are forgiven, three times you will start making enemies.

You don't have to go to every social event

Especially during 'O' (Orientation) week, but try to do a couple.

Understand student bathrooms

Have your own wash bag containing all your necessary toiletries. Wash your towel regularly. Invest in a pair of flip-flops (reduces fungal infections). You may also be on a roster for cleaning duties.

Get a bicycle and use the recreational facilities

It is cheap, portable and convenient. You will need lights, helmet, lock and pump. Use the gym and sports clubs to meet other like minded students.

Talk to your Instructors

It makes for better learning and a possible letter of recommendation later.

Be an activist (non-militant)

Take a stance on some issue. Look at the issues the student union is combating and pick a couple to stand up and speak out about.

DO NOT keep your negative feelings to yourself

Talk to your friends. They may be feeling the same emotions, especially home sickness. There are student counsellors on campus and there will not be a problem they have not heard about and have a strategy to suggest.

Give University a chance

Think of the big picture (a qualification), take time to settle in, have fun and meet new people (some may become friends for life).

Have a Plan B

Depending on the university, up to a quarter of university students 'drop out' in their first year. Give it a chance but have a back up plan just in case.

Paying for a University Education
(Scholarships, Sponsorships and Student Loans)

Because going to university can be very expensive, universities may have limited places for students who cannot afford to pay the full cost of their course. These places are available for eligible students and the government, organisation, business, sponsor, or university may pay all or some of the cost of the courses.

If you cannot afford the full cost of the qualification you want to achieve, you should go online to the web site of the university you are interested in studying at, to search the different ways students can fund their courses. You may need to research how scholarships work, how to get a sponsor and if any type of government loan is available. If you have any questions try to talk directly to someone at the university.

A government loan for university study is usually paid back to the government once you have finished your university degree and your income has reached a certain level. With a scholarship or sponsorship you need to fully understand how you are required to pay back the cost of getting your qualification and repay the belief they have shown in you.

How to Apply for Financial Assistance

Go online to the Department of Education website in your Country, State, or Province and search for Student Loans. If government loans are available the web site should tell you how to apply for them.

Careers Advisors at your school or college should be able to inform you if they are aware of any scholarship or sponsorship programs, what the requirements are and how to apply for them.

NOTE: You need to give yourself enough time to complete the application process BEFORE you start your studies.

Please Understand *EVERY* Agreement you are Required to Sign

It is very important that you research, read thoroughly and ask questions about anything in the agreement *BEFORE* you sign.

Talk to advisors at the university

They know all the 'ins and outs' of loans, what difficulties you might face in the future, what happens if you withdraw from subjects, what if you leave university temporarily or forever and many other common problems.

My Working Life

The Secrets of Successful People

"The greatest mistake you can make in life is to be continually afraid you will make one." Source: Elbert Hubbard US Writer

As long as you do the best preparation, your mistakes should be small. Learning from mistakes is what moves the world forward.

"In order to succeed, your desire for success should be greater than your fear of failure." Bill Cosby US Comedian

Your desire for success is going to help you make better decisions than your fear of failure.

"The best revenge is massive success." Frank Sinatra US Actor and Singer

For anyone who has ever disrespected you, their jealousy of your success is the best revenge.

"If you can solve your problem, then what is the need of worrying. If you cannot solve it, then what is the use of worrying. Santideva (Buddhist Monk)

If the problem can be solved all that matters is the time it will take. For a problem that can't be solved concentrate your energy on a different approach.

"When you truly love something, it just drives you and gives you incredible energy for what you are doing." Sam Johnson, Volunteer Army, Christchurch NZ

Your passion will give you the energy to succeed.

"The number one reason why people give up so fast is because they tend to look how far they still have to go instead of how far they have gotten." Vaibhav Shan Poet

Any project that you have a true passion for is a journey. Think of it like a triangle. The work and effort you put in at the start (the base) and lessons learned along the way make the rest of the journey to the top a little easier.

"Successful people aren't smarter or luckier than others. They just try so many different things and fail until something works out." Amir Khella Entrepreneur, Designer, Start-up Advisor

They have learned enough from their past failures to make this one succeed.

"Every great dream begins with a dreamer. Always remember, you have within you the strength, the patience and the passion to reach for the stars to change the world." Harriet Tubman (1820-1913) Humanitarian

You have the same ability to do what great people in the world (past and present) have done. But you need to have the deep rooted passion, drive and determination to succeed.

Steve Jobs Explaining Success
Founder and former CEO of Apple Inc.
These are some of the insightful things he said;

"You can't connect the dots looking forward; you can only connect them looking backwards. So you have to trust that the dots will somehow connect in your future. You have to trust in something; your gut, destiny, life, karma, whatever. This approach has never let me down, and it has made all the difference in my life."

Trusting that something in life has a plan and purpose for you and you are not on this planet just making up the numbers, is extremely important. When you feel that you know what that purpose is, you should try and reach the best possible conclusion.

"If you don't love something, you're not going to go the extra mile, work the extra weekend, or challenge the status quo as much."

If your heart is only partly involved in something you are not going to be as focused, excited or energetic and it will take a lot longer to finish it.

"You've baked a really lovely cake, but then you've used dog shit for frosting (icing)."

Every part of your product needs to be the best it can be, because the parts that have less quality lower the quality of the overall product.

"If you keep your eye on the profit, you're going to skimp on the product. But if you focus on making really great products, then the profits will follow."

If you just want to make money, the quality of your product will suffer because you will take shortcuts. Top quality products will sell themselves once people use them because they will tell people they know how good your product is.

"I'm convinced that about half of what separates the successful entrepreneurs from the non-successful ones is pure perseverance."

Believing in your product, adapting to changes, and finding another option when your original idea has not worked out means you are determined to succeed and that dogged determination will see you take your product as far as you can.

"Creativity is just connecting things. When you ask creative people how they did something, they feel a little guilty because they didn't really do it, they just saw something. It seemed obvious to them after a while."

This happened to me. Read the section 'Writing this Book'

"Here's to the crazy ones, the misfits, the rebels, the troublemakers, the round pegs in the square holes, the ones who see things differently - they're not fond of rules. You can quote them, disagree with them, glorify or vilify them, but the only thing you can't do is ignore them because they change things. They push the human race forward, and while some may see them as the crazy ones, we see genius, because the ones who are crazy enough to think that they can change the world, are the ones who do.

People who think differently and do things differently are usually the ones who come up with different approaches to a common problem. They are not afraid to challenge conventional thinking and because of that, they are the innovators of the world and move it forward.

What are the Common *Qualities* of Successful People?

They Had a Vision
Every successful person remembers the occasion when they found a 'gap' in the market, a new product came to mind, or they developed a system to streamline a process. The story on how you got started is very important because it gives hope to other people, that they might too stumble across something one day that puts them on *their* path to success.

How You Think, is Everything
You have to try and have a positive attitude all of the time. This trait has to be one of the most important in the whole list. You will have days when things don't go so well but it is important that you are always positive in front of people you are employing, otherwise their attitude will be affected. You will also need to learn how to deal with rejection and people's negative attitudes because the moment you have doubts about your ability you will lose focus and motivation.

They are Creative
Creativity is an ability to think 'outside the box' and invent and develop new solutions for everyday tasks and products. Creative traits include having imagination, entrepreneurial spirit, courage and boldness. If you have none or only some of the above creative traits, you will need to find a work partner that does.

They Take Action
Goals are nothing without action. They are just dreams. It is that simple.

They Decide what their *TRUE* Dreams and Goals are
Write down your dream and develop a plan with your mentor (if you have one) to reach it. Your ultimate *GOAL* is to *REALISE YOUR DREAM* but you need to have little goals along the way. You are breaking down your dream into measurable 'bite-size' pieces of achievement that track your progress. Then you have to picture the path to your dream, workout a suitable time-line and maintain the burning desire to make your dream become a reality.

They Communicate Well

Being able to communicate with the people in your team and the people who you are going to depend on to bring your dream to reality, is one of the most important traits you need to develop and develop quickly.

You need to be able to listen and understand what someone is saying not only in their words but also the information they are not saying (implying). This is called 'reading between the lines'. You will also need to demonstrate empathy. This is when you identify and understand another person's point of view or situation. To speak effectively you should keep your head up, look at the person and speak clearly. Try to use their 'language', not yours. Successful people develop and nurture a network and they only do that by treating people openly, fairly and many times firmly.

They know how to Sell Themselves and Their Ideas

Selling is a skill that is very important and has helped many people around the world become successful. Selling should *NOT* be about pressuring people or selling products or services by devious means because you probably will not get any 'repeat business. Selling is explaining the reason(s) why your customer is better off with 'your' idea/product/service over other market competition.

The Principles of Selling are also knowing how to;

- Negotiate (so that each 'party' receives a positive result),
- Deal with people who tell you "NO" (not everyone needs your product right now),
- Remain confident and maintain your self-esteem when your sales pitch is rejected,
- Communicate well with a wide range of people (to build long term relationships and repeat business)

Getting someone to agree with you and buy your product/service is only *HALF* the battle. The other half is to convince them to stay with your company and give you their repeat business. This is where 'Customer Service' is so important (Read the chapter on Customer Service).

They Keep Records (Diary, Notebook and Notepad)
In addition to the usual office paperwork and financial records you should keep the following;

The Work Diary is to provide structure in your own life and is used to keep track of things you need to do during the day and also to keep track of basic expenses and bills to pay.

The Notebook is something you always keep close. There may be more than one notebook because ideas and thoughts can come to you at any time. As soon as the idea or thought comes into your head you need to write down a few words to jog your memory later. If you don't do this, it can be very frustrating trying to remember the thought later on, because you have been thinking about a lot of other things since.

The Notepad is for you to take the notes from your notebook and expand the idea into a more defined form ready to be discussed with other people or transferred to a computer.

They Set Ambitious Goals
Once you have an idea what exactly it is that you want to achieve, you need to get the best possible team of people around you. Maybe you want to have the best product, the fastest, the cheapest, the biggest etc. You have to decide where you want to end up. *That* is your goal. Knowing what your goal is will motivate you and help you to make better decisions. By working *backwards* from your ultimate goal (and ultimate success) you, your mentor and other professionals can fine tune the paths you must take along the way.

They Make Plans
With your team, set each long term and short term goal with a timeline for completion and break the path to each goal into achievable pieces. You will also need to have an organised daily routine. Plan each day's work activities and do not allow distractions (this is where an office person could be useful).

They Understand *HOW* "the System" works

If you are part of an established organisation and are looking to succeed within that organisation, you need to know who the decision makers are and who has the power and who knows what is really going on. Mentors are often valuable sources of information regarding company politics. They are well connected people who have the inside knowledge on how to succeed within the organisation.

They Start Early (5-6am)

When you get up early you can take advantage of a quiet household in order to plan your day and do some basic work uninterrupted. Organize yourself a good nutritious breakfast and clear your head by reading the paper or watching some news and *then* think about and plan the day's activities. Answering emails or messages early will distract you from your breakfast and planning. Wait until you get to work.

They *DOUBLE-CHECK* Everything

Mistakes cost time, money and reputations. They may not always be able to do it themselves but there should be procedures in place where staff are trusted to make sure information and products are always checked for correctness and quality before they go into the outside world.

They Know When to Take Smart Risks

There is no reward without risk. Do not be afraid to try different things. Do the research and calculate the risk. The willingness to take a chance is a trait of highly successful people. If it doesn't work, calculate what went wrong and learn from the experience.

They *NEVER* Stop Learning

If you are taking action to achieve a dream outside of your current job, you may find that there are skills you could do with that will help you save time and money. For example; my computer skills are beginner to medium, but I realised if I could get the skills to eliminate the 'hard returns' in my manuscript I could save myself about $200 and a week of time. That skill is another little goal working towards my dream and also provides me with more motivation. It is funny how once you are out of school you realize how enjoyable learning can be.

They are *NEVER* Too Proud

Successful people generally know they owe a lot of their success to others. It is very important that as their success develops, they can still admit to themselves and others they made a mistake, they can say 'sorry', to still ask for help and to laugh at themselves.

Once a successful person develops a 'chip on their shoulder' and starts believing they are better than others around them, things can fall apart quickly. They soon lose the respect of their workers and any arrogance or lack of communication skills will have a negative effect on their business.

A friend of mine used to work for Richard Branson at the Virgin Records Megastore in London. Richard Branson visited one day and had been briefed on everyone's name and position in the store and my friend said he did not get one name wrong. It has always stuck in my mind that someone with that amount of success has taken the time to correctly identify the people that work for them.

So that's some of their secrets. What else can you learn from their examples?

Surround Yourself with Great People

There is a saying "You can't do it alone." If you have ever seen an awards ceremony, you know that the person receiving the award usually has a lot of people to thank. These people are the trainers, the workers, the mentors and friends and family who constantly support them. The talents of these people include; being positive, supportive, inspiring, talented, knowledgeable and while being successful in their own right they aren't on a stage getting an award.

Find a Mentor

If you are working in an established business already, talk to someone you look up to and see if they are interested in being a mentor and helping you 'fast track' your success. If you are looking at starting your own business a mentor can help to shorten your learning curve, open your mind to new ideas and possibilities, identify opportunities and advise on how to promote yourself. Having a person or business to 'mentor' you, develop a plan and introduce you to business contacts means you have a solid foundation and therefore 'comfort' in the knowledge your dream is progressing. Mentoring is a proven concept not just an idea.

"Mentoring is a brain to pick, an ear to listen, and a push in the right direction." John Crosby

"A lot of people have gone further than they thought they could because someone else thought they could." Zig Zigler Motivational Speaker

Keep up your Energy

It is not enough to have goals and desire to succeed. Your body needs to be able to handle the routine of your day. That may mean 12 hours or more of work. You need to eat often and eat healthily. Drink plenty of fluids. You could also take a multivitamin to boost your nutritional intake and you also especially need to make sure you get enough sleep.

Balance Your Life

Your path to success is important but you need to take time in your day to meet with friends, appreciate your partner, play with your kids, exercise and just relax and wind down. Your life needs to have the minimum amount of stress possible. With a balanced life comes happiness. This is the ultimate secret to life.

Develop an Effective Network

Talk to those people who you and your mentor determine can help make your dream become a reality. These people have the skills and the industry contacts to help you reach your goal.

Protect your Ideas and Products

There is an unwritten law where professional people and companies do not talk about the details of your conversations and your ideas with other people, unless they have your permission. However not everyone is trustworthy and you may want to protect your ideas in the form of a confidentiality agreement (written up by a lawyer) and get professional people and business to sign it before any discussions. This document can used against any person or business in a court if they tell unauthorised people about your plans.

Do Not Sweat the Small Stuff

Work out what is important in your daily routine (and your life in general) and give it the priority it deserves.

Remain Humble

Never forget where you came from and the struggle it took to be successful.

Promises Define Your Character

If you can't keep them, do not make them.

Be Professional and Responsible at *ALL* Times

Lastly and probably most importantly, you need to have a professional and responsible attitude 24 hours per day if you want to be successful.

You need to know that if you do anything 'stupid' and it gets out into the public arena, that lack of judgement can erase all the hard work you have put in to becoming successful. Your credibility, profile and reputation can be destroyed and people who were close to you now will not want to be near you because you will damage *THEIR* reputation.

Employment

In order to have a successful life, a job is very important. Earning enough money to not only survive, but save for the future means you have good feelings about yourself (self esteem) and your ability to provide for yourself (and family) while enjoying your life. If you know what type of work you want to do then you have a big advantage over someone who is struggling to decide what career to choose. You can research the basic qualifications you will need, enrol in the course(s), get qualified and work your way up to the top of that profession.

For someone who is unsure about the type of career they want, it usually means trying different jobs until they feel they know what they want to do.

I am a person who, after leaving the Navy, had no idea about what work I wanted to do. I left with NO qualifications, had no career plan and for the next 25 years had over 30 different jobs. The shortest period of work I had was for 3 months and most of the time I was termed a 'casual employee' which means I did not get the benefits of a 'full-time' employee. I have never had a life-long passion about a particular type of work. Right now, my focus is getting the information in this book to young adults all over the world but that takes time and I still have to survive by doing two 'casual' jobs.

Whatever type of work you end up doing, whether it is a career or a short term job, it provides you with money to survive. You have to remember unemployment numbers are high and there is always someone out there who wants *YOUR* job.

If you have no idea what career you want to do, ask yourself:
What are you passionate about?
What are you good at?
What do you know a lot about?
What is your dream job?

Ask friends and family what they think you would be good at.

Do what you can to earn money to survive
It may be at working at a supermarket or fast food restaurant or mowing lawns. It will pay the bills until something better comes along.

There is always some else who could do your job
Do it to the best of your ability and the boss will not have a need to replace you!

Find something you love to do and get paid doing it.
Life is too short to be working in a job that you don't want or like. You are going to be working for 50 years so you might as well find an area of employment that you think you will love doing.

Your first job is often not the one you want to do for the rest of your life
Start out in the job market and then look around for the right job while you are doing your current one. Don't wait until you get fired, laid off or made redundant before you start looking. People who already have a job and can show that they have been reliable and loyal employees, have a better chance of getting a better job elsewhere.

Your only guarantee of job security is if you own the company
Job security is not guaranteed in today's financial environment. Companies are always looking to cut costs and boost profits and staff are usually the first to go. The remaining staff will be expected to work harder. Their only reward is that they still have a job.

Remember casual workers usually get 'laid off' first
Casual workers are employed at high production and busy times of the year. During quieter periods their working hours are the first to be cut in order to protect the full-time worker's jobs.

Get a part time job for a talent or interest that you have
If your main job does not challenge you or use your skills but it pays the bills, consider finding a part-time job as well that you are interested in. The part-time job is a foot-in-the-door to the full-time job you really want, and if the main job for whatever reason is no longer available the part-time job will cover your basic expenses.

Positive things employers want in their staff

These are the qualities that employers want: dedication, they start work on time or a few minutes early, they are willing to learn and to learn quickly, they work hard, they give 100%, they are not afraid to ask questions, they follow workplace procedures and they do as they are told.

How to help protect your job

You can protect that job to the best of your ability by turning up early to work, doing as you are told, completing tasks properly, asking questions when you are unsure about anything, following procedures, filling in all paperwork properly and being skilled in a number of areas in the workplace.

You may need other skills in order to get a job

Research the job market and think about doing training courses in a field that interests you. Such courses could be a truck licence, first aid certificate, workplace health and safety, forklift licence, upgrading your computer skills etc. The more skills you have, the easier it may be to find a job.

Motivation and attitude are important

Being determined to make something of yourself, to reach your personal goals and having the right attitude will help you to get where you want to be in life.

Multi-skilling and flexibility are two desirable qualities a person can have

Being able to adapt and work in different areas and at different times is a quality employers really like in their staff. If you are trained in a number of areas of a workplace you will be more valuable to a boss, than a person trained in only one area. Ask your boss if you can be trained in other areas as well.

Work out the strengths and weaknesses of your character

Things you are good and not so good at. Areas you want to improve in. It gives you a true personal sense of who you are and the direction you want to go. Put the positive ones on your CV.

Site Inductions are very important.

Safety in the workplace is very, very important and it is the law in most countries for anyone new in a workplace (employee or visitor) to be made aware of any dangers within the site. If you have not been given a site induction, ask to be told about; any hazards that exist, personal protective equipment available, the chain of command for reporting incidents, paperwork you are required to fill in, the whereabouts of safety equipment, emergency procedures, muster points when evacuating the work site and anything else you need to know when at work.

Time management is a very important skill to master

This is best done by making a list of required tasks from the most important through to the least important (priority). Work your way through the list obviously completing the most important tasks first. Being distracted from your work will prevent you from getting the jobs done on time.

Concentrate on one task at a time and always do a task to the best of your ability

This way you are not distracted from the task you are doing and can concentrate on putting in a quality effort. Multi-tasking means working on two or more things at once. If you do this at work you are more likely to make mistakes that cost the company time and money as well as damaging your reputation by being unreliable.

What to do if you are required to do a few things at once?

This can be managed in a couple of ways. Ask for some help to get them done. If there is no help available ask your boss, or work out for yourself which task has the higher need (priority). Then start with the most urgent task down to the least urgent task and do not allow yourself to be distracted.

Try and break hard tasks into smaller easier tasks

Sometimes you have or are given difficult things to do. Take some time to think about how to go about completing a difficult task. You *DO NOT* want to be wasting time from any misunderstandings. You need to have a clear idea on what the finished product/service/task should look like. Putting the task down on paper may help you. If you get stuck, ask the right questions of the right people.

'Cover your back' at work

Some workers don't like people who love their job and work hard because it makes the lazy ones look bad in front of the boss. They may blame you for their mistakes to destroy your reputation. This can be difficult to manage, because if they know you've complained, they can make your life miserable, especially if the boss doesn't care or does nothing. You may just have to put up with it until you can be moved or find another job. Meanwhile, be very wary of any information or instructions you receive from anyone other than your boss.

Learn how to provide excellent customer service

It's the customers who provide your pay, so always treat them well. 'Customer' means anyone who comes to your workplace, not necessarily to buy something. Be polite, ask them if they need directions or help.

If you are in a sales job, talk with your boss on what extras the company can provide and/or the lowest price you can go down to in order to make the sale. You won't need to go to that limit often, but occasionally you will come across a person who is very good at getting a bargain (negotiating). Look at the next chapter and find out more ways to provide great customer service.

You will *NEED TO LEARN* to *TAKE ORDERS* from your boss

Until you are the boss of your own company or are in the management level at work, you will be required to take orders. Get used to it.

Never beat your boss at anything or make them look bad in front of people

Your working life will be worse off.

'Sky-larking' (fooling around) in the workplace is dangerous

Save the fun for when you finish work.

Disciplinary action at work.

On any work site you need to know about the 'safety' document (it may be called the 'Code of Conduct' or something similar) that outlines what is and is not, appropriate behaviour in the workplace. There can be many times in a workplace whereby incidents happen and disciplinary action is appropriate. They will range from a minor occurrence to something that can be extremely serious and put lives at risk. Examples are; not following orders and procedures, not filling in paperwork properly, not doing proper checking, inappropriate behaviour towards other staff, damaging equipment, improper use of equipment, fooling around, dangerous driving and accidents that could have easily been avoided etc.

If you are employed on a 'casual' contract or part of a work agency you may lose your job immediately if the occurrence was deemed a serious one. For those people employed full-time or permanent part-time, there are protocols based on your employment contract that should be followed by your employer. For example, if a minor rule breach was observed, after a discussion about the details you would probably get a verbal warning. Any future breaches of the same rule or something else will probably lead to a written warning and a meeting with a variety of people to work out why it happened. You should be made well aware of the problem you caused and you may be given extra training so it does not happen again. If an incident you are involved in happens a third time, after another lengthy discussion you may lose your job or you may get your second and last written warning.

It really all depends on the nature of each incident and the ones that follow, as to how it will ultimately be dealt with. When starting any new job, as part of your site induction, you should be made aware of the disciplinary system procedures at your workplace.

Do Not accept workplace harassment and bullying

Tell the person that you feel like you are being bullied and it is not acceptable. If it continues tell your Workplace Health and Safety Officer. They may be required to keep a record of the complaint and aim to resolve it. But they need proof that it is happening. DON'T keep it inside as it will stress you out. Tell your parents as soon as possible, especially if it is your first job and you are inexperienced at how to handle the situation.

How to provide instructions

Being polite but firm is the key. A good idea is to tell a person the reason why they need to do something. They will be more willing to carry out the tasks required. For example; 'John, a truck is turning up in a few minutes. I need you to unload it as quickly and as safely as possible, as it has to go back out on another job…Thanks.'

If you work for a 'family' business

There can be two sets of rules, one set for the family and a different set for the workers. If family members argue, avoid becoming involved, and don't take sides no matter who you think is in the right or the work environment may become very uncomfortable for you.

Do a 'Small Business' Course

This will teach you how to become your own boss and how to manage your responsibilities of owning a business. It will also help you understand the problems your boss has to deal with, and that will make you a better employee.

Beware of drinking too much at work functions

Especially if you are female. It will be the talk of the workplace the next working day. Have a professional attitude even at workplace parties.

Always, *always, always,* ask for a Letter of Recommendation for any paid work you have done if you think you did a good job.

Whether it is for one hour, one day, one week, one month or one year, always get a Letter of Recommendation (reference) from your employer. This is an important piece of documentation that outlines how long you were employed and how you performed at the job you just left. To help you get another job you should show these references on any future job applications. Keep these recommendation letters with your CV. As you change jobs, address or phone number update your CV and remember to scan it onto a USB stick and keep it safe.

Customer Service Skills

"You are what you repeatedly do. Excellence is not an event – it is a habit"
Aristotle (Greek Philosopher)

If you can learn as much as you can about how to give excellent customer service then not only will you develop a great reputation but it may lead to bigger opportunities.

Customer Service is extremely important. If you have ever had a bad customer service experience then you probably have not been back to that store because of how you felt at the time. You need to know that a customer is not only someone who buys something, they are also any person who comes into the place where you work. They maybe there for an appointment, to compare prices or to offer a service. They are there for a reason and as soon as you make them feel welcome, you can find out what that reason is and either help them yourself or you can direct them to the area or person concerned.

Products and Feelings

The thing a person buys is a 'means' to the feeling they get when they use it. For example, people like their coffee a certain way and when it is made that way they have a fantastic feeling. Once they find a person or place that regularly provides the 'perfect' coffee and the feeling that goes with it, they continue to go to that place. What helps even more, is when the customer service they receive, is better than they expected. After a while they will become known to the staff and may get priority service and occasionally, a free coffee. All of a sudden it becomes a part of their daily routine and the shop benefits because of the 'repeat business'.

You are the *'FACE'* of the Company

The owner owns the store, the manager runs the store but **YOU ARE THE FACE** of the company because the customer's view of the business you work for, comes down to the image of you that they see, and how much you are able to assist them. For this reason it is very important that your personal grooming and choice of clothing is in line with the stores policy. As a side note; anyone who is 'just looking around the store' should still be viewed as a potential customer and as a customer service representative of the store you should be doing as much as you can to assist the person make a decision to purchase. Ask the person who trains you how the company expects you to do this.

Training

Any job that has you dealing with people usually means you will receive some training by the supervisor/manager/owner of that business. A good business will have positive proven customer service techniques that they want you to use to develop their business further. Once a person has a good experience as a customer it makes it very easy for them to come back to the same place again. If there was a 'WOW' factor to your service, they will almost always tell their friends. The place where you work benefits and you get to keep your job and maybe get promoted.

Basic Customer Service Skills include;
Introducing yourself and paying attention to the following;

a) **Grooming:** Hair and nails tidy, use of deodorant, removal of inappropriate jewellery (piercings, rings etc). You are there to sell the business' image *NOT* your own.

b) **Clothing:** If it is your own clothing it is best to use plain, neutral colours. Advertising names or 'slogans are not appropriate. Cover tattoos. Again you are promoting the business *NOT* yourself.

c) **Acknowledging the Person:** Let them know you see them waiting and you will attend to them as soon as possible.

d) **Smiling:** If you are smiling it makes it a lot easier for people to come to you and ask for help. This goes with politeness.

e) **Politeness:** Have a calm, friendly voice and show that you are willing to help them.

f) **Needs:** Sometimes customers themselves don't know what they need. Ask them questions to find out how they use something then direct them to the best matching product.

g) **Knowledge:** If you don't know what *ALL* the stores products do then you can't match a customer with the right item.

Customer Complaints

It takes a lot of courage and effort for people to make a complaint. The reason why people complain is usually because the 'feeling' that they got from the product or service was not as good as they expected. Some people will just put it down to experience while others can't be bothered taking the time to phone or drive to the store to get the complaint sorted. You now know when you are faced with a person complaining about a product or service, it is a serious issue. How you handle that customer is going to affect their overall view of your stores customer service and they may praise or 'bad mouth' your handling of their complaint to their friends.

How to Deal with Complaints

Usually the customer needs to bring the receipt (along with the item) back to the store from where it was bought. Without the receipt there is little proof where the item was bought. However you should find out your stores policy on product returns that don't have a receipt.

What is also very helpful is the store-person's name who sold the customer the product or service so that person may attend to and correct any mistake that they made.

Customers hate being passed from person to person and repeating their complaint over and over. If you do not know the original salespersons name and want to help the customer to resolve their issue it is probably best to start by writing down the basic facts of their complaint. Then if you have to pass them to someone who can handle the complaint better, the facts you wrote down prevent the customer from having to repeat themselves.

For a complaint to reach a successful ending ideally the customer has to leave with not only the complaint being sorted out properly, but a great feeling to go with it. This can be done by rewarding the customer for the effort they made to bring the complaint to the stores attention. Maybe something unexpected like a small 'freebie' that gives the customer the feeling they did the right thing and will still come back to the store in future. Talk to your 'boss' about extra service you can provide.

How to Write a Good Cover Letter

There is no point applying for full-time work that you have no skills or interest in, hoping that someone will employ you. That usually leads to a waste of time and effort on your part and you probably won't even be contacted to say your application was unsuccessful. You should start out working in an area that suits your current skills or interest. You will need to give examples of those skills and your depth of interest in your Cover Letter and on your CV/Resume.

Getting a job interview is a big deal especially if it is the career you want to be in. But in order to get that interview you need to develop not only a good CV/Resume but also a good Cover Letter that makes you stand out from most other people applying for the position. Each Cover Letter will change with every job application because of the different aspects of each job. It may even be necessary to alter your CV slightly for each application (resume) to closely match the responsibilities required of the role.

You should know that a CV (curriculum vitae) is a document that has *ALL* your work history and that a 'Resume' contains just the relevant work details for the job you are applying for. At school you might have been taught how to put together a CV/Resume, but it is the Cover Letter that you send with those documents and job application, which will determine whether the person looking to hire someone, is going to look at your complete application.

The Cover Letter and application details are the ones that usually get you into the *FIRST* 'short listed' pile of applications. This is because the person looking at the application has no time to look at all the resumes' sent in from other applicants.

Your resume' will get you into the *SECOND* short list of applicants for the interview stage and is still very important because if you cannot put together a good resume' that backs up the details in your Cover Letter, you will probably not be chosen.

The business or organisation wants a worker to help their business be profitable and grow or to improve or expand their services, so they'll be looking for somebody who shows that they have some natural talent as well as a good attitude. You should learn as much as you can about what their company does so that your Cover Letter will show that you are interested in *their* interests.

Do an online search or visit their office and pick up their brochures in preparation for a possible interview. At the same time you should try to find out the person's name who is 'screening' people for the job. Find out the correct spelling of their name, double check it and address your Cover Letter to them personally.

You must be absolutely honest. Don't claim experience or skills you don't have to try to get an interview, because you'll soon be found out, and that will be the end of it.

A *GOOD* cover letter needs to grab the reader's attention and show how you can help the company through your youth, enthusiasm, willingness to learn etc. Whether it is a posted or an online application you should keep it to one but definitely not more than two A4 pages. It should:

- Include your contact details – your name (as you like to be known), your mailing address, your email address, and mobile phone number;
- Show that you want the job because the work interests you;
- Address each of the requirements mentioned in the job advertisement. Show in one or two sentences how you satisfy each of them;
- Show as much as you can that *your* interests match *their* interests. If they make products; tell them why you are interested in their product, and what experience you have that is relevant. If they provide home care to elderly people; tell them about the work experience you have had or that you've cared for you grandmother for many years. If you don't have any actual relevant experience be honest about that and show that you have the personality and desire to learn.

- Employers will be interested in what you've done in the past that shows your potential. Maybe you were captain of your basketball team, so you have leadership skills and are a team player. You like rod fishing, so you have patience. You organise your church's youth dances, so you care about people. And so on...
- You should also include any dates or times that you will not be available for an interview.

For more information on Cover Letters and CV/Resumes' search online or seek advice directly from Job Search Agencies.

Job Interviews

Being selected for a job interview is a very good thing. Out of all the people who sent their resumes' in for the job, you were one of the few people selected. Something in your resume attracted the attention of the person looking at all the other applicants. But you are only halfway there. No interview should ever be taken lightly.

Even the less wanted jobs have a lot of people applying for them because the days of a guaranteed job for life have disappeared. You should approach any interview like you would for a big exam: Research and Practice. Get friends or family to help. *You can never over prepare for a job interview*. You should also have your own questions to ask the interviewer.

Before the Interview

Do know something about the company
Research the company. Visit their website. Find out about the company's past performance, vision for the future, the amount of staff employed, where other branches are located and turnover of annual revenue. Find out the name of the interviewer and do not forget it.

Speak to the 'Contact Officer' *BEFORE* submitting your application
You should make every effort to speak with the 'Contact Officer' nominated in the job advertisement *BEFORE* submitting your application. This is the opportunity to ask questions such as:

- Could you describe the typical duties for this position?
- Will weekends or shift work (evening/night) be required?
- What are the expected hours and days of work?
- Are there sickness and holiday entitlements?
- How many people in the team/business?
- Is car parking available?
- Is the position full-time, part time or casual?

If you don't like the answers to any questions, you may change your mind about applying and save everyone from wasting their time and efforts. On the other hand, it is a good chance to make a positive impression with a key person in the recruitment process. Quite often the Contact Officer will be one of the main people at the interview.

Do practice an interview situation with your parents or friends

This will get you used to focusing on the interview process. Take the opportunity to practice by dressing appropriately and using the information in this chapter to polish your listening and answering skills. Even talking in front of a mirror or recording yourself can be helpful.

NOTE: Behavioural interviews are becoming increasingly popular. You may be asked to recall a situation in your life or previous employment where you developed and applied a certain skill the interviewer is looking for.

Do dress appropriately

Dress according to the job position. If it is an office position, smart business dress is appropriate. If the position involves manual labour, smart casual dress is appropriate.

Do not take any food or drink into the interview

If you spill it, you may be viewed as clumsy. Water is always provided.

Do not use your phone during the interview

If you use it, it shows you can be distracted when you are supposed to be concentrating. *SWITCH IT OFF.*

Do not arrive late

Being late tells the interviewer you are not an organised person. Allow plenty of time to get ready, travel to the interview and if necessary find a car park.

At the Interview

Do be polite
People form impressions about others within the first few minutes, so it's the initial contact that is critical. Say hello Mr/Mrs/Ms ...and shake hands using a firm grip. Call a person by their first name *ONLY* if you are told to do so.

Posture
Don't slouch, sit up and look the interviewer/s in the eye. Don't mumble. Speak clearly

Do try and stay calm
We know it is easier said than done. It is okay to let the interviewer know you are a little nervous. When asked a question, take a moment to breathe before you answer the question. An interview is not a school exam and is not a memory test! You can take notes in with you, or even better, have a copy of your application and CV to look at. You can always take a sip of water to give yourself more time to reply. It is also okay to ask for a question to be repeated – especially if it is has several parts to it.

Do pay attention
If you do not pay attention this tells the interviewer you are easily distracted which means you may be unproductive and unsafe in the workplace.

'Fuzzy' Resume or CV facts
Not being able to provide simple time-lines to questions or being unclear about previous employments tells the interviewer you have lied on your CV. This quickly destroys your honesty and credibility.

Do not interrupt the interviewer
Listen to what is being said and wait until they have finished talking before answering.

Do not answer questions with just a 'Yes' or a 'No'
You should provide details, but keep to the point raised.

Do not talk too much

An employer wants you to demonstrate drive, passion and how you can contribute to the company. They do not want you to have outbursts of emotion and go to areas away from the subject.

Do Not say bad things about past employers

Briefly describe any previous employments and the amount of time spent there. Explain the duties you were doing as part of your job, if they relate to what you are expected to do at the one you are being interviewed for. Talking badly about previous bosses will not help you because the interviewer may ring them for a reference and it means you may talk badly about the person interviewing you now.

Questions to ask at an Interview

- Will someone explain how to do the job – give a hand-over, or is it work it out as you go along?
- Is there opportunity for training and professional development?
- What sort of career opportunities are there within the organisation?
- Are there any expected changes to the organisation in the near future?
- When do you hope to have the position filled?
- Is there a 'trial' period and how long is it?

It is far more effective to weave your questions in amongst the interview if possible and instead finish with a summary statement of 30 seconds maximum.

This is known as the *'recency effect'*. The interviewer(s) will remember the last thing you said – it leaves a lasting impression, so choose your words carefully!

After the Interview

If you didn't get the job

Call the 'Contact Officer' and ask why you weren't successful. It may be just that someone else was better qualified, but ask 'Was it anything to do with my interview style?' and if there is anything you could do to improve your chances next time?

Paying Tax in Your Country

For anyone that has ever left school and got a job, the payment of tax can be a mystery. The tax system can be very complicated. At the very least you need to have a *basic* knowledge of the tax system in your country and I strongly advise you to do a bit of research, otherwise it can cost you time, money, a lot of inconvenience and in extreme cases heavy fines and jail.

As a general rule, **your employer pays all required tax for you** during the year. Therefore the money you get in your hand or your bank account each time you get paid (pay day) should already have any tax taken out.

> **Wages =** Money you receive based on the amount of hours you work.
> **Salary =** You receive the same amount of money each year regardless of the hours you have worked.

Generally the more money you earn, the more tax you pay

Your country's tax system is governed by the 'tax year', which may not be the same as a normal year (January – December). For example in New Zealand the tax year is 1st April – 31st March the following year. In Australia the tax year runs from 1st July – 30th June the following year.

You need to know what the 'Tax Year' is in your country so you can meet your tax requirements on time.

When you start working you may just have your wages as income which makes understanding the tax system a lot easier. Your first year tax return is usually the simplest it will ever be. Paying tax becomes much more difficult as you get older because you will usually have other sources of income. This extra income can be from investments you have made, another job, money you have won or government benefits.

You will need to do some research on any expenses you may be able to claim back from the government. Any money you have paid for work related items may be one expense you can claim back.

It is best to apply for a Tax Number as soon as possible

When you begin any new job you will be asked for your tax number. You may have to fill in a form and will need to enter your tax number. This is a number that is given out to you by the tax department and stays with you for life even if your circumstances change.

If you do not have a Tax Number you may be taxed at a much higher rate until you get one and you may not be able to receive certain government benefits until you have one.

To apply for a Tax Number, go online and type into your favourite 'search engine' Apply for a Tax Number. Click on your country's tax website and look for the appropriate 'section' to begin your application.

Your Payslip

Every time you get paid, you should receive a 'payslip' that shows you how many hours you have worked, how much money you earned, how much you paid in tax and the amount of any other deductions that has come out of your pay.

End of Year tax requirements

In some country's your tax is worked out automatically by the tax department at the end of the year and you will only be contacted if there is a change to be made. The most common ones are underpaying or overpaying tax.

At the end of the tax year in other country's, you may have to submit a tax return (a large form) to your country's tax department. You will have to supply all relevant information such as how much you earned in the past tax year, how much tax you paid and any other information the tax department requires. Your employer from any jobs you have had during the year may give you or send you a document that has the basic information on it. You will need to collect all these forms and transfer the information from them onto your government tax form.

Tax returns can be done by yourself but as they get more complicated it may be best to spend a little money and get a professional person to do it as they understand exactly what you may be able to claim. These tax returns usually have a submission date and you may be liable for extra costs if it has not been received by the tax office past a certain date.

All tax paperwork must be completed *TRUTHFULLY*

There may be severe penalties including jail if it is shown you have deliberately tried to deceive the tax department.

Note: The government tax office will have a requirement where you must keep all tax paperwork (including receipts) for a number of years (usually five or seven). It is a good idea to scan all relevant tax paperwork and put them on a USB stick with all your other important documents for safekeeping. Keep the USB stick where it is **completely safe**.

Superannuation (Retirement Fund)

Superannuation is another name for savings for you to use when you have retired. That's many years away, so why should you be bothered with it now?

It's because the *GOVERNMENT* of your country *MAY* have a system whereby money is paid into a super fund for you, and this fund usually has tax benefits. Those tax benefits and better returns (interest) over time are far better than bank accounts for saving money. The big problem is you usually can't take any of the money back out again before you retire except under some special circumstances – like, you're dying.

You need to do some research to find out if the government of your country has such a fund that you (through your wages or salary) or your employer pays into, to help provide an income for you once you are much older and have finished your working life.

If your government *DOES* have a fund that collects money to help you later in life then I *STRONGLY SUGGEST* you find out as much as you can about this fund. Do some research and find out who pays into it and how much, the account numbers, the amount of money in the account, contact phone numbers and web site address, if you are allowed input into where the money is invested.

If there is *NO SUCH FUND* then your retirement income will be *ONLY* be made up of your savings and any 'pension' fund the government provides. Any government pension will only cover the bare minimum of living costs. There will be no extra money for luxuries or holidays so it is up to you to save as much money as you can and invest it for the future.

Another point to consider is people of your generation are living longer. That means when you retire around 65, you have the real potential to live for another 25 years. That is way more than the current life expectancy for males and females.

Barely surviving on a basic government pension (if one is available) for 25 years is not going to be fun.

As soon as possible you need to work out how much money you think you will need *EACH* year in retirement.

It is advised that you start saving for retirement as soon as possible
Then you need to work out how you are going to achieve that total amount of money. I urge you to seek the help of a financial planner in order to help you reach your financial goals.

Workplace Health and Safety (WHS)

Being safe, not only at work, but wherever you are, should be your main priority. If you are injured how do you look after yourself and pay your bills?

In many countries there are laws regarding Workplace Health and Safety (WHS).

Employers (Owners/Managers) usually have a legal duty known as 'Duty of Care' to take all reasonable practical steps to provide a facility, plant, equipment and environment that is healthy and safe for workers, visitors and contractors. They should also have to ensure the safe use, handling, storage and transportation of dangerous substances (chemicals) as well as provide information, instruction, training and supervision to their workers.

Workers are usually required under the same laws to also;

- have a 'Duty of Care' to act in a way that does not place their own health or safety or that of any other person at risk;
- obey all directions issued by an employer and a Health and Safety Officer;
- stop work on the identification of an unsafe practice ;and
- report any accident, incident, dangerous occurrence or near miss immediately.

It should be the law to provide every new employee or other person (such as a contractor) in a workplace with a Site Induction. For someone who is working on a work site for a short period of time a basic site induction will be done, but for a new employee a more in depth induction is required.

A Site Induction is designed not only to show the employee around the site but to point out hazards that exist and the controls in place to prevent injury. It should point out emergency equipment, where it is located and muster points in case of evacuation. It may include filling in paperwork such as tax and bank account forms as well as the issuing of clothing and PPE (Personal Protective Equipment).

All staff need to be aware of the importance of all documentation on a work site and the requirement for documents to be filled in accurately. You should be satisfied that if the law, company procedures and rules are followed by everyone, you can return home safely at the end of the day.

Workplace Health and Safety means:
1) identifying a hazard and reporting it to your supervisor;
2) working out how much risk of injury there is;
3) controlling the risk of a hazard through:
   a) avoiding it;
   b) eliminating it;
   c) isolating it;
   d) substituting it;
   e) engineering controls;
   f) administrative controls;
4) inspecting (monitoring) the controls in place through inspection and the collection of data and to see how effective those controls are.

Note: Only the first item is your responsibility. Items 2,3 and 4 are normally done by a Health and Safety Officer.

A HAZARD is anything likely to cause injury or harm to you or anyone else.

RISK is the degree of likelihood that a hazard will ***ACTUALLY*** cause harm.

The purpose of a Risk Assessment is to work out the degree of likelihood a hazard will *actually* cause harm.

It is especially useful when one or more hazards are found, as it will help to determine the priority status of each hazard through the degree of risk it poses.

Hazard Classification:
Physical: lifting
Chemical: gases, fumes, liquids, fire
Ergonomic: things like tool and equipment design
Environmental, such as noise, lighting, temperature, dust
Radiation: X-rays, microwaves

Psychological: includes bullying, shift work, discrimination
Biological: plant and animal materials; electrical shock
Mechanical: machinery and plant

Hazardous substances can enter the body through:
Inhalation (respiratory), ingestion (swallowing), absorption (skin) and injection.

Effects that hazardous substances can have:
Asphyxiant (suffocation), irritation to skin, nausea, vomiting, inflammation (blisters), asthma, nose bleeds, anaesthetic (feeling no pain), chest pain, damage to nervous system (brain) etc.

Risk Assessment
Thorough risk assessment requires training and experience, and is usually done by specialists. But that doesn't mean you can or should ignore obvious hazards. You *must* point out anything that you think is a danger to you or your workmates.

Because there can be many hazards in a workplace, an assessment needs to be done to see which hazards have the highest risk of causing injuries. The hazards having the highest threat to the health, safety and welfare of the employees are given priority in regards to controlling those threats.

When doing a risk assessment there are a number of things that will be considered; the location of the hazard, how many people are exposed to the hazard, how often they are exposed and the length of time of exposure.

There are numerous risk assessment tools available but each tool has the same objective, which is to put the risk into a category of Low, Medium, High, Extreme, Critical or Catastrophic classification.

Controlling the Risk
The process of controlling identified workplace risks begins with the WHS committee discussing on how best to remove or minimise the risk. The most common process is to use the 'ladder of controls'.

The 'ladder' is designed to approach the method of risk control in a logical manner:

- Can the hazard be avoided?
- Can the hazard be eliminated?
- Can the hazard be isolated?
- Can the hazard be substituted for something safer?
- Can an engineering control be introduced to make the hazard safer?
- Can an administration control be introduced to make the hazard safer?
- Can further training be introduced to reduce the risk of exposure to the hazard?
- Will the wearing of appropriate Personal Protection Equipment (PPE) reduce the risk of exposure to the hazard?

Hazard Register

A Hazard Register should be kept by the Workplace Health and Safety Committee to keep all records of identified hazards and their control measures in one system of referral. All identified hazards need to be monitored over time, results collected and compared to the earlier results in order to maintain appropriate control measures.

Any workplace is a 'fluid' system, meaning things like staff, equipment, tools, work methods and laws are always changing. The workplace needs to have risk control measures that are monitored regularly, to keep the workplace safe.

Injury Compensation in Your Country

You need to research whether your country *HAS* a scheme that helps people if they are injured at work.
Injuries at work cost the company and the person involved, time and money. It is in the best interests of the employer and workers to have a safe workplace.

Some countries have a government injury compensation scheme that helps people who are injured at work (and maybe away from work) with financial assistance, medical bills and recovery services.

The role of any injury compensation organisation should be to educate people to prevent injuries happening, to get them appropriate treatment if an injury does happen and to assist the person with their recovery so that they can return to their usual daily activities as soon as possible.

Any money you may receive as a result of a work place accident is usually limited to a percentage of your income, so if you are on a tight budget already you could be at risk of money problems.

Because there are so many different factors that apply to each case, every claim should be looked at on an individual basis.

In the event of *ANY* injury happening at work, the person receiving the injury should be required to report it to a nominated Health and Safety person at their work. For any major injury that occurs to a worker, an employer may be required to report the injury to an outside organisation within a certain time frame.

Seeing a doctor to determine your injury
A medical assessment by a doctor will be necessary to determine the extent of the injury received and whether it is covered by any injury compensation scheme. Once a diagnosis has been made, it can usually be determined what treatment needs to be provided and how long the person will need to recover from their injury. A copy of the doctors notes will usually be submitted with any claim form (the workers and/or employers).

Your responsibilities when making any claim

The injured worker and the employer are usually required to fill out separate documents (forms). Both parties should be required by law to only provide information that is truthful and there are usually severe penalties for making false statements.

NOTE: By working with their employer to make the claim together, an injured person can collect all the correct information and lodge it at the same time therefore speeding up any claim process.

It is in the worker's best interests to do exactly as they are directed by any doctor or health professional so that they minimise their recovery time and get back to work and full income as soon as possible.

As an injured worker you may have also an option to take legal action against an employer as a result of their 'negligence'. This is something you will need to research.

Money Matters

About Money

Money is the 'commodity' that brings us together and tears us apart. If you have plenty of it then life can be very exciting because you have an opportunity to experience many aspects about life few other people get to experience. But having a lot of money brings its own share of problems. There are many stories of people coming into money suddenly (lotto wins, family inheritance) and three or so years later, they have absolutely nothing left.

For most people, having enough money to maintain their idea of a comfortable lifestyle is a constant struggle and they live from week to week on their pay packet with nothing left over. *YOU* have to manage your money better than that.

The decisions you make regarding your money will determine how wealthy (rich) you become. You need to become knowledgeable in regard to earning, spending, saving and investing it. Money should be working for you, *NOT* the other way around.

I estimate that in my life so far I have wasted over $150 000 through my own ignorance, not asking the right questions, not doing enough research and not seeking professional advice. ***DO NOT MAKE THE SAME MISTAKES I DID.***

READ THIS SECTION THOROUGHLY AND OFTEN.

80% of what you buy should be for what you **need.**
20% should be for what you **want.**

Everyone is after your money
Thieves and scammers want to steal it. The government, and 'local authority' want it to pay for the services they provide. The police take it as fines when you get caught breaking the laws. Every business wants it so that they can stay in business. You work hard for your money so make sure you are the one who gets the benefits.

"A fool and their money are soon parted" Old proverb

All adults have been a fool at some stage. They fell for a scam, they did not ask the right questions, they did not read or understand what they were signing, they did not get the right advice or they did not do their research and as a result they got 'ripped off', paid more than they needed to, or they simply lost their money.

Prioritise your spending- the essentials *first*

Spend your money on what you *NEED* to survive. Food, shelter and bills first before you spend money on things you *WANT.*

There is a fine line between living for today and saving for tomorrow

This is the problem that everyone faces. Do I live my life today because I might not live long *OR* do I give up a lot of fun and excitement now and save my money for the future? No matter how much you earn, there never seems to be enough to save for a 'rainy day'. Control your spending to what you *NEED* by budgeting. Refer to the chapter on 'Budgeting'.

Buy things by using your head and *NOT* your emotions

Emotional expenses (wanting it, not needing it) and buying on the 'spur of the moment' are the ruin of most budgets.

Do not let your eyes be bigger than your bank account

Having nice things takes time. Don't buy things that put a strain on your budget. Live within your budget and you will be fine otherwise the downward debt spiral can take hold quickly due to high interest and excess fees... and it will stress you out.

You have to understand you need to start at the bottom with basic practical stuff and work your way up to the nice, expensive stuff

The people who have brought you up started out the same as you are now, except back then times were a lot tougher. There was no instant information at their fingertips, no convenient mobile phones and no social media. They had to work hard to put food on the table and to get ahead in their life they may have had two jobs. When they moved out of home they had to search for cheap, useful furniture to get by with. As they got older, they got more settled somewhere and their wages improved, they bought better quality things.

You have to start out the same because you are probably going to be in a renting/sharing situation for a while before settling down and any new stuff you buy now is going to take a battering.

You get what you pay for
Generally the better the quality of an item, the higher the price you pay. Budget or entry level things are cheaper because of the lower quality. A good rule to remember is "buy cheap, buy twice".

BUDGET, BUDGET, BUDGET
Weekly, monthly, three monthly, six monthly and revise it. Know how much money you potentially have for the week and based on what you are earning now, you can work out longer budget periods.

Set yourself short (three months), medium (six months-one year) and long-term (two-five year) goals
Check those goals regularly and work out what action you need to take to reach those goals.

Keep a calendar and write down when payments are due
This helps organise your life. Late payments for bills often attract penalty fees.

Read and understand your bank statements
Understand where your money is going and ask the bank to check any problems you find.

Keep receipts from the major things you buy
You will need to produce them for refunds or warranty issues.

Keep receipts for work related items; tools, clothing, training courses etc.
You may need to produce them at tax time to get them deducted off your 'gross' tax amount.

Keep all major receipts, warranties, tax information, insurance policies

Organise the items in large envelopes or an expanding file. It is a good idea to photocopy cash register and credit card machine receipts as they can fade over time and may not be readable later.

Save 10% of your weekly income into an 'Emergency Fund' that is not readily accessible

Put the money directly into a 'term deposit' account for a higher rate of interest. Holidays, nights out, 'strapped for cash' for the week, are not emergencies. It is for when you are out of work and have run out of money in your usual day to day and savings account. *ONLY THEN* do you access it to pay your bills, pay the rent and eat.

The *REAL* interest rate

With any interest rate you need to know that your country's inflation rate needs to be taken into consideration. Say your bank is giving the money in your 'everyday' account an annual interest rate of 2%. But your country's yearly inflation rate (the overall price increase in the cost of living) is 3.2%. That means each year your money loses value. One way to get around this is to have just enough money in your everyday account for your expenses and to put the rest of your money into your Emergency account and Savings account on a term deposit for a higher rate of interest. As the value of your accounts grow through added savings and interest, you can look at other investment options for an even higher rate of interest. A professional financial advisor is the best person to talk to when investing a larger amount of money. As an example, a balanced investment portfolio may return 10% in a year and if inflation is 3.2% then the value of your money has actually grown by 6.8% whereas money in a standard bank account will have lost value if the inflation rate is higher than the banks interest rate.

New stuff loses its' value very fast

The value of new items can drop by 25% to 50% as soon as you walk out of the showroom. This is the amount that makes up the store's overhead costs and profit on the item.

Avoid on-line shopping sprees
The best way to purchase items is still to go along to a shop, feel the product, assess the quality, check the warranty, and talk to the sales staff. With on-line items you pay the money up front which has its own risks. Is it a scam? What guarantee is there I will actually receive the product?

Shop around for the best prices, but 'let your fingers do the walking' (phone)
If you need something, ring around a few stores or search 'online' to get the best value for your money.

Learn to negotiate, not just money but terms of contract to suit you
As a buyer (consumer), you are in the strongest position at the point of sale, just before you hand over the money. Ask for a reduction in price, better payment terms/warranty or added accessories.

It is a big risk to lend money to friends or family
For some reason they never feel they have to pay it back. There is always a bill or a 'toy' that is a higher priority. You will feel foolish and awkward asking for it. Written agreements don't seem to make much difference.

Before you sign any loan agreement
You *MUST THINK* about how you are going to pay off the loan if your income suddenly 'dries up' due to job loss, accident etc. There is insurance you may be able to get that covers unforeseen circumstances but it is always best to wait until you have saved the full amount before buying the item.

Insurance to fit your needs
As you get more modern possessions, start a family and have a secure career it is important to protect the things you have already and rely on. Insurance is designed to protect your savings and to provide financial assistance when the unexpected happens. Review the need for the following insurances every six months throughout your life; Life, Income, House and Contents, Car and Health and Funeral. Compare different company's services with their prices to find the best 'value for money' insurance company.

Reduce and eliminate debt as soon as possible and don't built-up debt

Interest that builds up through missed payments and late payment fees will set you back financially and it will stress you out.

Don't always believe what people tell you regarding investments

Do your research. Get a few professional opinions. Previous good results by a company are *NO* guarantee of future good results.

The secret is to 'make money work for you' not the other way round.

Once you have reached a high savings level you need to get that money working for you by earning good interest so that you can re-invest it to boost the amount of money you have. To start with, a simple term deposit offering higher rates of interest could be the way to go. As your savings increase over a few years you should seek independent financial advice on how to invest it for better rates of interest.

YOU NEED TO KNOW short-term investments are all about timing and that long term investments will usually give you more gains than losses over time *BUT* there is ***NEVER*** a *GUARANTEE*.

DO NOT put all your 'eggs in one basket'

This is a classic piece of investment advice handed on from generation to generation. What it means is that you do not put all your investment money into one thing. You spread the money you have to invest, across different things. You might put some of your money into shares, some more into property, or some more into a slightly riskier investment. But you do not put all your investment money into one thing because if that one thing fails, you lose a big, big, chunk of that money.

When you have saved some money (over $5000) and want to invest it, get some financial advice from professional people you trust. Talk to two or three companies for different ideas.

A car is *NOT* an investment

A car goes down in value as it gets older. In fact a brand new car loses a ridiculous amount of money by the time you have driven it out of the car yard. You may get a long life out of a car and that will be good value for the money you paid. However, the one exception to the rule is, if the car is a *RARE CLASSIC* that appreciates rapidly in value ; *BUT* that is a *VERY RARE* occurrence.

Only in very exceptional circumstances will you ever be able to double the value of an investment in three to five years

Be very wary of people telling you it's easy to do. Get a second or third opinion. Do your research. Ask questions. Use your brain NOT your heart. *IF IT SOUNDS TOO GOOD TO BE TRUE THEN IT USUALLY IS.* Walk away and seek further advice. *DO NOT SIGN ANYTHING* until the opportunity has been fully checked out. You can 'google' anything and it can start you on the path of seeing how other people got rewarded or scammed.

To find out how long it would take to *double the value of any investment* (if it was left alone and you don't take any money out) divide the number '70' by the amount of interest offered on the investment.

If you are offered 6% then 70 divided by 6 = 11.666 (11 years and 8 months). If you are offered 10% then 70 divided by 10 = 7 years.

Be aware of people promising high returns over short periods of time (scams)

These people are very slick operators who are primed to say what you want to hear. *DO NOT SIGN ANYTHING* until you have done your own research. Get their name, company's name and contact details. There may be police operated 'scamwatch' hot lines available in your country to double-check if you could be the target of a scam.

Con men do not look like thieves

They dress well and say the things you want to hear.

Get your investments to mature (pay out) at different periods

Investments pay out at the end of their investment period. You may have the option of re-investing (rolling over) some or all of it to a future date if you don't require the money at the time.

Compounding interest is good when investing but bad when you have loans

Compounding interest on **investments** is when the interest earned is added to the amount invested, so you **earn more interest** on the interest already earned. That's very *good* for you.

Compounding interest on **loans** is when the interest charged is added to the loan, so you **pay more interest** on the interest already charged, and the interest might be calculated daily, not monthly. That's very *bad* for you. Avoid it by paying off the loan as soon as possible.

While in any phone conversation to professionals, customer service, or retailers

Always write down who you called, the time you called, the date you called, who you spoke to, prices quoted and any other general information needed. Take that information with you if you are intending to buy the product. If a different person is dealing with you at the store they will usually give you the price quoted by the person you originally talked to in the interests of customer service.

Reward yourself for the hard work

For just plain surviving and for sticking to your budget, allow yourself a small luxury item (jewellery, a night out, tools etc.) every so often to boost your spirits. Look forward to the day you get them because they are your reward for managing your money well. However, you should not spend more than you can afford at any time.

Do you really want to be paying off a holiday six months after you have had it?

Have the holiday only after you have saved all or most of the money.

Shop around for a good financial advisor and lawyer

You may not need one for a little while, but once your savings increase to investment levels, a financial advisor can start a portfolio and help you reach your goals. A lawyer can start legal processes and check paperwork before you sign it.

Professional Advice

The first meeting with someone professional to advise you on money matters is usually free as they need to judge whether their services are actually going to help you. Because you are young, are seeking knowledge as well as the right answers, they will usually be happy to provide excellent customer service to get your repeat business.

If you do find yourself in the following situation where you:

- fear opening your mail from companies you owe money to;
- are afraid to answer the phone because it might be someone wanting money;
- are thinking about getting one loan to pay off all your debts;
- are finding the interest rates on your loans make it very hard to keep up payments,

then you may need the help of a debt management company. Go on-line and search for a 'debt management' company in your area. When you ring them to book an appointment they may ask you a few questions. When you arrive at an appointment you need to make sure their services are actually going to help you. Have a list of your own prepared questions and do not sign anything until you get it checked out further. You must be clear on knowing exactly what you are required to do and the penalty they will impose on you if you don't do it.

Do not sell high value items at auction

These are houses and expensive vehicles. An auction will only get you the next value after the second highest bidder's price which may be thousands of dollars below what the highest bidder would have actually paid, *plus* you may pay high rates of commission as well as added government charges (VAT, GST etc). Auctions usually attract bargain hunters. For more information on the 'bad' side of auctions go online and search 'auction pitfalls'.

Buying vehicles or homes at auction is a pressure situation

Emotional attachment to an item will empty your pockets beyond what you budgeted for – every time! If you are the highest bidder and you have second thoughts about what you have done *DO NOT SIGN* any paperwork. There is no legal requirement for you to do so. Walk away. If you do sign paperwork at auctions there is usually *NO* legal cooling off period.

Cooling off periods

With most written contracts there is a cooling off period, meaning if you go home and something doesn't feel right about what you bought or signed, you can take it back within a certain time (for example, one to five business days) and get a refund less a small fee.

A cooling off period may *NOT* apply in certain situations

In some countries, buying a house at auction and buying a new car (the two most expensive purchases you will ever make) are *NOT* covered by a cooling off period. So *BEFORE* you make a bid at any auction or buy a new car you need to do a lot of research comparing prices and conditions, and work out in your budget exactly how much you can afford to offer. You should definitely check out whether a 'cooling off' period is available if you are thinking of buying *ANYTHING* expensive.

I do not recommend you buy any *high priced* items at an auction until you fully understand how the auction system *actually* works (there are a lot of traps) and you have thoroughly compared prices on similar items and done your homework on the item's condition.

Even if you have said *YES* to something at an auction it does not become yours until the *OFFICIAL* paperwork is completed. Until you sign that *official* paperwork, you can always walk away if you are having second thoughts. The auction people won't like you doing that but it is your right to do so. Nothing is certain till the official paperwork is completed.

Be very wary buying residential property 'off the plan'

'Off the Plan' means you pay a deposit up front for a building that has not been built yet. Generally, the developers are waiting for enough interest from people and their deposits to fund the project. There are stories of these projects not starting and people losing money, or if they do get built, you often don't get the quality the glossy brochures showed. Wait until it's built, then inspect the finished product and wait for those owners who over committed their money, to sell and you may be able to 'snap up' a completed unit for a greatly reduced price.

Beware of the Lifestyle Trap

The lifestyle trap of the western culture is the 'I want it now' syndrome. You see it everywhere; the expensive cars, the big screen TVs and all the latest toys and gadgets. All of these things are bought to feed people's egos and to make other people including family and friends believe they are successful in life. But the catch is they don't own it. The bank or loan facility who gave them the loan (or credit card) does and those people will be paying high rates of interest and penalty fees if they miss a single payment.

The idea of buying and enjoying nice things before full payment (delayed gratification) is increasingly popular and many people fall into the trap of making the purchase based on emotion (they fall in love with it) and not with their brain. They don't read or understand the paperwork they are signing and they under-estimate the risk of not being able to afford monthly payments. Sometimes it takes an unforeseen bill like a dental emergency to put their budget out. There may be advertisements on TV where you ring a phone number to help you get out of the debt cycle by freezing interest and stopping harassment from debt collectors. Increased personal debt is becoming a major problem in societies.

The risk of making late or no payments at all leaves you open to harassing phone calls, threatening letters, a debt collector calling round to your home, repossession (taking back) of the goods you bought and a bad credit rating which will affect your ability to get future loans. Do this enough times and you will need to declare bankruptcy. Refer to the chapter on Bankruptcy.

Before you buy anything big that is new, or for a high price, *THINK*, could something less expensive do the same job? If the answer is 'Yes', then search out that cheaper option and avoid being tied down by debt repayments.

Do not spend money to impress other people

There is nothing wrong with having nice things if you can afford them. There is nothing wrong with having a mortgage (loan for a house), as long as it is manageable on your income and you have appropriate insurances in case of unforeseen circumstances. Debt is okay if it is attached to something that will *INCREASE* in value (appreciate) over a medium to long period of time. This is called an *INVESTMENT.* Examples are property, shares, gold and other precious metals.

At this stage in your life you do not need to spend more than $3- 4,000 on a car if you are paying for it yourself. A car is designed to get you from A to B and yes, it requires you to look after it. You can search 'Cars for Sale' ads in your local paper and pick up a reasonable car for about $4,000 including getting it checked, serviced and registered (see the chapter 'Buying a Car' in this book).

It makes no sense to buy an expensive car and pay it off over a number of years including interest. When you want to sell it, you will have paid much more than what you will get for it because the vehicle has gone down in value. That is not the way to 'get ahead' in life.

The Debt Cycle (This is Important)

Many 'western' countries are better off than many other countries around the world because they enjoy a high standard of living. The basic needs of life: food, clothing, shelter and transport are in good supply and easy to get.

The life you have now is so much easier than your parents ever had. Technology has made things so much simpler through microwave ovens, mobile phones and the information available through the internet.

The nice things in your bedroom and parents' home give you a false sense of security of how easy life can be. You have little idea of the struggles that your parents have been through over the years to get where they are today. You weren't there when they first moved out of home and they had to start out with basic second hand furniture in a flat that may have been cold, damp or small. The excitement they had was because they were now away from the rules of their parents and were now free to live their own lives.

The *BIGGEST THREAT* to you having enough money for the future (financial security) is *GOING INTO DEBT* and being trapped in a 'debt cycle' because of non-investment purchases. This means you buy and pay off things that go down in value. This is called *'BAD DEBT'*. You will be paying loan or credit card interest on top of the purchase price while the item goes down in value. *GOOD DEBT* is the opposite. You purchase things that go up in value while you pay them off. Their value is worth more than what you will eventually pay for them (an investment).

You need to remember that *'good'* second hand appliances like a washing machine and fridge are also a good investment but for a different reason. They make your life easier. The purchase price is a lot lower than a new one and you usually get a long life from them if you treat them well.

The Different Cycles of Debt

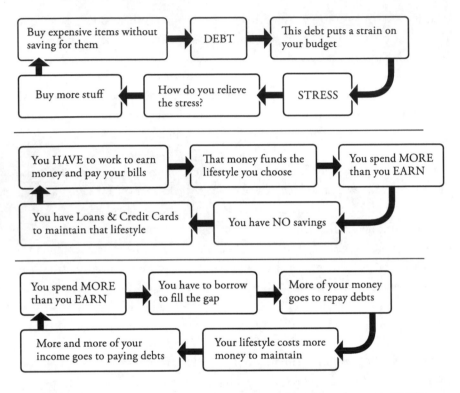

| Buy expensive items without saving for them | → | DEBT | → | This debt puts a strain on your budget |

| Buy more stuff | ← | How do you relieve the stress? | ← | STRESS |

| You HAVE to work to earn money and pay your bills | → | That money funds the lifestyle you choose | → | You spend MORE than you EARN |

| You have Loans & Credit Cards to maintain that lifestyle | ← | You have NO savings | ← |

| You spend MORE than you EARN | → | You have to borrow to fill the gap | → | More of your money goes to repay debts |

| More and more of your income goes to paying debts | ← | Your lifestyle costs more money to maintain | ← |

Get out of Debt:

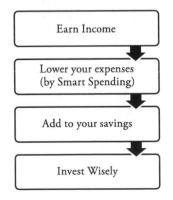

Earn Income

↓

Repay your debts wisely

↓

Lower your expenses (by Smart Spending)

↓

Add to your savings (Invest wisely)

Avoid Debt:

Earn Income

↓

Lower your expenses (by Smart Spending)

↓

Add to your savings

↓

Invest Wisely

The debt cycle starts with borrowing money to live the lifestyle you **THINK** you deserve and being in debt can lead to unhealthy levels of stress. As mentioned in the chapter 'Beware of the Lifestyle Trap' you have to start with a basic lifestyle now and through hard work, training courses and work promotions you can get to the point where you can afford better quality items for your home (just like your parents have done).

It is called '**delayed gratification**'. Delayed gratification means waiting until you have saved all or nearly all of the money for something that you need and *THEN* buying it. The added benefits of this method are that it forces you to stick to a budget by setting money aside for the item and when you have saved the money you may decide that it is better spent on something else because your priorities have changed.

Some of your friends may decide that they cannot wait till they have saved the money. They want to have nice things now and because it is human nature to take the seemingly 'easy path', they decide to take advantage of seemingly 'cheap' loans that may be available, or use a credit card, and not worry about the consequences.

YOU HAVE TO BE SMARTER THAN THAT. When you buy things on a credit card or take out a loan, it means sometime in the future you will have less money to spend than you earn because you are having to pay back your loans. The more money you borrow now means less money for you to spend in the future.

You have to *AVOID BAD DEBT* and secure your financial future by saving. You cannot rely on a job for life, the government or your parents to bail you out if you make bad financial decisions. **Knowledge is Power.** Use that knowledge to make better decisions when investing your money.

Questions you should ask yourself before going into debt over a purchase:

- Can something second hand or cheaper do the same job?
- How will I afford the payments if I am injured or out of work?
- Am I buying this item because I *WANT* it or because I *NEED* it?

If you still insist on buying the item, *READ & UNDERSTAND* all documents *BEFORE* you sign the loan to pay for it. If you do not understand what the documents say, ask questions and be prepared to walk away (with a photocopy) to think about it or seek another opinion. Once you sign, *YOU ARE NOW IN DEBT.*

The thought that "I can always sell it if it doesn't work out" is not a good idea because it may take a long time to sell and the price you will get could be less than half what you paid for it. Losing money does not help your financial future. Forget what it cost (that was the store's price with profit margin added), you will only ever get what someone else is willing to pay for it.

Pay off your debts wisely

Work out how much interest you are paying per year (annum) on each loan or credit card. For example you may have one loan at 12%, a loan through a big department store at 22% and a credit card at 15%. You can approach this two ways. Talk to the loan provider who has the lowest interest rate and see if they will loan you the amount to pay off the other 2 companies you owe money to. This means the others with high interest payments will be paid and now you only have one big loan at the lowest interest rate. The other way to do it is to pay off the loan with the highest interest rate first, then the loan with the next highest interest until you are left with only the one loan at the lowest interest rate. There will be other ways to reduce your debt and I strongly recommend you seek professional advice on how to do this that best suits your current situation.

There are a few ways to get out of the debt cycle – stop using your credit cards, cut down on your mobile phone use, don't start any new loans, and pay off as much as possible of any existing loans and credit cards.

*It is much better to not get into bad debt in the first place by always spending less than you earn by saving and investing the rest. **IT IS THAT SIMPLE.***

Debit Cards and Credit Cards

Debit Card

A debit card is used to buy (purchase) items with money *YOU have already saved* and that money is in a bank account attached to your debit card. As long as you have money in your bank account, you can buy items *up to that amount* with the debit card.

There are usually different fees attached to debit cards. Fees such as an annual fee and when the card is used to purchase an item (also known as 'transaction fees'). Check with your current bank for more information regarding the different fees and how they can be reduced.

Once you get comfortable living within your budget and operating a debit card, you may decide to operate a credit card.

Credit Card

A credit card is used to buy (purchase) items with *somebody else's money, not yours, and you have to pay that money back, with interest.*

BEFORE you get a credit card you need to work out whether you actually *NEED* one. You can do this by checking your history on how you spend your money and what you would be using one for. But *beware,* it is very easy to spend money that is not yours and your credit rating will suffer if you do not pay all the money back plus interest.

A credit card *uses the bank's money* when you don't have enough of your own and it can be used for big or small purchases (over $10). *But you need to pay this money back.* You need to be really organised with making monthly payments when you have a credit card. The best way to do this is to get your bank to make a regular payment from your debit card account to your credit card account for you. This is called a 'direct debit' and there is usually a fee attached to this.

You can set a limit for yourself as to how much credit (the bank's money) is available to you. $1000 is a good amount to start with. Once you have learned to pay that amount back to the bank, you can apply to the bank to have your 'limit' increased.

Many banks will try to trap you like this. You have shown you can manage your $1000 limit on your credit card because you bought some things and paid them off regularly. The bank sees this but they don't wait for *YOU* to ask for an increased limit based on your budget. They will send you a letter or e mail, automatically increasing your credit card limit to $5000 or more. The danger is that you overspend because you've not been keeping a watch on how much you are using the card, then you can't pay it all off at the end of the month, and interest is added, and the interest can be very high (15% or even higher).

Banks make their money on interest payments and late fees and they want you to over spend. Do not be tempted to spend this extra money unless you absolutely **need** to.

Stick to your budget

Some credit cards offer interest free periods, for example 55 days for you to pay off the amount purchased. This means after 55 days, you will be charged interest on the balance owing. Credit card statements in some countries, by law have to include a warning on making only minimum monthly repayments, telling you how long it will take to pay off the credit, and how much interest you will finish up paying. For instance, a credit balance of $800 requiring a minimum monthly payment of $30 would take nearly three years to pay off and the interest would be over $160.

Also most credit cards have an annual fee attached to them. Research a number of bank (or other) credit cards by picking up the brochures that tell you all about them. You could also go online and enter the card's name and the word 'complaints' to see which one has the least complaints and issues.

Be very careful about rewards programs. They are designed to keep you loyal to the operator of the card and as well as other companies and the rewards are often less than 1% of the amount you spend.

CREDIT CARDS NEED TO BE USED WITH EXTREME CAUTION.

It is very easy to spend money that is not yours. Debit cards however, give you the same advantage of shopping without having to carry a lot of cash, and it's only *your* money you have available to spend. To learn more about credit card debt go online and search for 'secrets your credit card company doesn't want you to know'.

DID YOU KNOW

Many people who have a credit card, may never pay it off. All they will do is continue to make the minimum monthly payment required by the credit card company. They will be stuck with the debt for longer and pay even more interest. As they buy more things and interest builds up further, the monthly amount payable increases as well as the time it will take to pay off the credit card. It is a vicious cycle that you do not need in your life.

Your Credit Rating

As you go through life, you will build up a credit rating. Basically your credit rating is about your reputation as a borrower and the likelihood of you paying back the money you borrowed. The better the credit rating, the more likely you are to get approved if you feel the *NEED* to borrow money.

When you start out on your own, you generally won't have a credit rating so the main information organisations will want to know when you apply for a loan is, "How are you going to repay the amount of money you borrowed?"

Having a job and a regular income (wages) makes paying back any borrowed money easier but it all depends on your budget. Does your budget have the room to make regular repayments in addition to the money you need to survive? There may be a section in the forms to fill in when making an application, that shows the lender you can afford to make repayments.

Information from a wide range of organisations including loan companies, utility companies (power and phone) etc will be collected and sent to a credit 'agency' in your state, province or country to build up a credit report on your financial history. You will then be assigned a credit rating. Other companies can then access this information to determine their risk before giving you approval for loans etc.

Obviously if you don't fully pay back any money you've borrowed you will have a bad credit rating (as well as losing the item you bought) and any loans you might apply for in the future (such as a house loan) can be rejected because of the bad risk you pose when it comes to paying back money.

Bankruptcy

'Bankruptcy' basically means you cannot pay back money you have borrowed. As a result of not being able to meet all of the required payments on things you have purchased, you enter into an agreement where you (the debtor), signs over control of your money and all your possessions to an outside person or company (trustee). The trustee usually takes control of everything you own except clothing, household appliances, government superannuation (if any) and car (up to a certain value), Then your possessions get sold to pay the people you owe money to (creditors).

What you get in return, is protection from legal action against you by the people you owe money to. There are some big restrictions for those people who get into a lot of debt and have to declare bankruptcy. Firstly, bankruptcy once declared, usually lasts for three years (it may be longer in your country) and on regular occasions throughout the bankruptcy period you may be required to supply a lot of information regarding your income, identification and residence. Any change to your personal information such as income, address, phone numbers, next-of-kin or your job, needs to be sent as soon as possible to whoever has control over your finances. There are usually heavy penalties if you do not do this.

Any house you own or have a share in will be sold. Any car over a certain value will be sold. Any money you get from lotto wins, TV game shows, family inheritance, or other sources, will be used to pay off your debts. Any item of value that is given to you will need to be 'handed over' as well. If your income is over a certain level, you will usually be required to make payments to the people you owe money to (creditors). Your ability to travel overseas or run a business will have restrictions, as will the job you are able to do if you have a real estate licence, builder's licence, security licence, liquor licence or tax licence etc. Your credit rating may be affected for up to seven years or longer. This means you may not get any loans that you apply for because you are viewed as a bad risk.

I had to declare bankruptcy once. My problems began when I had made a good profit on a block of land I purchased. Wanting to reward my friend of 18 years who had helped me, I suggested we might form a partnership if there was an investment opportunity. We found an ocean front apartment that we thought would be a 'good investment'. The friend moved to another city soon after and apart from signing the bank paperwork, I never heard or saw anything of them again.

The building work on the unit was poorly done and there were other problems so we could not rent it out. The 'friend' did not pay their share of the mortgage, my income dropped due to a back injury soon after the first payment so from day one I was in heavy debt to the bank. My mistakes: I did not do enough research, I did not get quality, independent professional advice, I did not have income protection insurance and I did not read the document's fine print. Being under a bankruptcy meant I had to live very simply on a very basic budget. I managed to get through, mainly because I know how to budget my money...but it was not easy.

DO NOT LET THIS HAPPEN TO YOU

For further information in your country go on-line and search 'Debts and Bankruptcy'.

By having a budget, saving some money each week and not spending money on unnecessary things, you will be well on the way to 'getting ahead in life'. If you start to feel any bills and loan payments (I hope you don't have loans) are becoming harder to pay, you will need to make changes to your budget. Once debt takes a hold of you, it can be very difficult to get out of.

If you find you are having trouble paying your debts talk to the loan payment companies and ask if you can reduce the monthly amount you owe them.

Try to pay off *ANY* debt that you have, within the interest free period or *AS SOON AS POSSIBLE.*

Get a Better Price (Negotiating)

Some goods and services that you buy have what is called a fixed price. That means it is highly unlikely you will get a reduction in price. Supermarkets, chemists, hairdressers, clothing stores, shoe stores, mechanics and other types of retail shops are examples. However, they may advertise periodic specials on TV, newspapers or on-line etc.

There are also plenty of stores selling items where the prices are not fixed and are able to be discounted. Big ticket items like cars, houses, furniture, electrical goods (fridges, computers, washing machines), but also markets, second-hand book and clothing stores tend to have discounts available. To get a discount not already available, you need talk to the right person to get the price down. This is called negotiating. Sometimes the simple approach works best when purchasing items by asking 'Can I get a discount on this item?' They may say 'No', but at least you found out. What if there was a discount available and you didn't ask? You would have paid more money than you needed to.

Tips for Negotiating

Firstly, when you are Selling
Honesty is always the best policy. Declare any faults with your product and have your price adjusted. You always feel better about being honest and your reputation and customer service profile stays intact.

When buying a used car or house
Get an independent professional to check it out first and based on any faults or problems they find, work out a better deal with the seller.

Talk to the person who *CAN* give you the discount
Not the person who can't. Introduce yourself, smile and find out their name.

Know what you need
If the sales person sees you are not sure about what you require, you could be walking out of the shop with goods you don't need.

Research the item you want to buy
If you are unprepared, sales people can take advantage of your lack of knowledge. Compare the price being asked to the same product in other stores or similar products in stock. Sometimes comparing products throws up an obvious fault in a store's pricing method.

Have something in common with the seller
This is a big factor. Find it quickly and discuss it with them. It builds trust and instead of seeing you as just another customer, for a moment, a friendship is developing. It is hard to say 'no' to a friend.

Listening and understanding to what the seller is saying
By paying attention they will feel respected and that builds trust. Get the salesperson to do the 'talk' about the item. This takes up their time and they will want to make a sale because of the length of time they 'invested' talking to you.

Mutual benefits
This is called a win-win situation. You win because you get a better price, but the seller has to feel like they got something out of the deal as well, otherwise they are not going to offer anything. You have to tell them how they benefit. Something as simple as their end of month sales figures will look better and you will tell your friends.

For 'tough' sales people
Ask them 'why are you selling the item at this price'? The seller then has to defend the price of the item and explain its price. This may become difficult for them and to make their life easier, they usually offer you a discount.

Learn to negotiate, not just money but other things to suit you
As a consumer, you are in the strongest position at the service desk, just before you hand over the money. Ask for a further reduction in price, better payment terms, warranty or added accessories.

Bulk Buying

Whenever you need more than one of the same thing (small or large), ask for a bulk discount. The second, third and fourth items sometimes come with great discounts. This also applies to a large amount of one thing (steel, material, flour, cereal etc).

'Bundling'

Is done in a similar way but the items are different.

Accessories

While the main item may have a fixed price there may be something free or heavily discounted that goes with it. A washing machine may come with a heavily discounted dryer, a car may have free accessories or a computer may have free software included etc.

Sales targets

At the end of each month salespeople are trying to boost their sales in order to meet or exceed their expected monthly targets. You have an opportunity to get the best deal at this time, even if the item is already discounted.

Seek legal and financial (money) advice

When you can afford to purchase a new car or a house, you need to get quality, independent advice from someone who is not going to benefit from the sale. There are so many tricks and traps agents or sales people use to get the sale. You can make sure you are getting a good price by doing your research to compare prices and features of similar products.

Your sales receipt

Record on the sales receipt the sales person's name and file it in a safe place in case you need to return the item under warranty. If you able to to use your receipts for tax purposes it is a good idea to photocopy cash register and credit card machine receipts as they can fade over time and may not be readable later.

Buyer Beware

There is a legal term 'caveat emptor' which means 'let the buyer beware'. Whether you buy goods from a store, 'second hand' or over the internet it is in your best interests to ask the right questions and satisfy yourself you are going to get a product that does exactly what you want it to do. The seller, however, usually has a legal responsibility where they must not tell lies about the item, it must not be faulty and it must do what it claims to do.

If you have problems with any products you have bought you should always try and get the problem sorted out with the manager of the store. You will need to show the *RECEIPT* to prove you bought the product from that store.

If your problem is not taken care of then go on-line and search for 'Consumer Affairs' or the 'Office of Fair Trading in your State, Province or country. These websites will be able to help you with consumer issues and also have an amazing amount of information that is designed to help people buy products with confidence. They also detail the tricks and traps some sellers may use to get your business.

A Budget
How to do one and how to keep within it

A good budget is working out where your money comes from and what you actually spend it on.

Where your money comes from is called 'income'.

When you spend your money, it is called 'expenses' or 'outgoings'.

Sources of income include earnings (wages) from any jobs you have, government benefits, money from parents, tips etc.

Expenses include rent, food, electricity, phone, transport costs, entertainment, loan repayments etc.

The more detail your budget has, the easier it is to understand where your money goes.

THE SECRET TO HAVING MONEY is to "Live Within Your Income". You cannot have a millionaire's lifestyle if you are earning a small to medium income. You have to start at the bottom like everyone else and work your way up to the big wages.

DID YOU KNOW even when you earn big money, a budget will probably still be necessary? This is because your tastes and lifestyle have become more expensive. In short, the more you earn, the more you tend to spend. The cask wine you had with your meal at university is now a reasonably expensive bottle of wine. The rent you paid for your room when starting out is now a mortgage on a house along with large running costs.

You can do a budget to cover a week, fortnight, monthly, three monthly and six monthly periods. You can put a lot more detail into the weekly budget because it is dealing with your life here and now, whereas the three and six monthly budgets are aimed at providing you with a general picture of where your finances will be, if you stay on the same track. However a lot can happen in your life in three-six months, so these budgets are subject to many changes.

The 'trick' to doing a budget is to under-estimate your income and over-estimate your expenses. By doing this you have a 'cushion' that can give you extra money each week and can gradually build up into a good amount that can be added to savings, used as a purchase to reward yourself or to pay an unexpected bill.

If you have a regular income, budgeting is a lot easier because you know how much money is available to you each week. What makes budgeting harder is when you have different amounts of money each week. This may be due to a number of reasons but casual and part-time work are usually the main ones, because the amount of hours you work may change from week to week.

Just by writing down how much money you have available from all sources tells you the total amount that is available for you to spend and save. You then have to list all the things you spend your money on and hope you have money left over because if you don't, you will not be able to eat well, operate a mobile phone, get to work or go out with friends etc.

The first things you should give up when you are on a very tight budget are entertainment and excessive phone use. You stay at home or you do things that do not cost much money. You still need a place to sleep (rent), you need food (although you can stop buying lunch), you need to get to work (transport), and you need electricity so the only things left are to lower your entertainment expenses and to stay within the plan you have with your mobile phone.

Do not spend more than you earn

If you do, the downward debt spiral can take hold quickly due to interest payments on loans and credit cards, excess fees on unpaid accounts, etc. Live within your budget and you will be fine.

Budget your expenses. Buy what you NEED, allow some entertainment expenses, put at least 10% of your weekly pay into a separate, untouchable account (investment account) for emergencies. Put 20% into a higher interest bank account to help you to save some money and bank the rest into your 'everyday' account bank account.

One way to force yourself from accessing any savings regularly, is to have somebody else, such as a trusted friend, also be present to sign the bank withdrawal slips. Hopefully they will question your need to have the amount of money you want to draw out.

Always buy things by using your head and *NOT* your emotions

Emotional expenses are those things you buy because you *WANT* them and are the ruin of most budgets. Grocery shopping without a list is a good example, because you buy what you *WANT,* not what you *NEED*. Having a list before you do any sort of shopping will save you a lot of money

Be money wise

Control your spending but spend it when necessary.

Buy items by asking yourself 'What do I need and how long do I want it to last'?

For example you might need a computer but there are so many different types available. Work out what sort of work you need to do on it, do some research yourself on-line or at stores and then find the computer that *FITS YOUR NEEDS*. Thinking about what you want it to do, how long you want it to last and your budget, will affect whether you buy an expensive version, value for money or a budget option.

You get for what you pay for

Generally the better the quality, the higher the price you pay.

For more information go on-line and search 'how to get more money out of your budget' Take a look at the websites listed. Some will have a layout (template) for you to get started.

Written Contracts

ANYTHING that you are required to *READ* and *SIGN* is called a Written Contract. A written contract can be loan agreements, employment contracts, insurance policies, bank account forms, investment contracts, legal documents etc.

Basically a contract is a written agreement between two (or more) people or business' that details what each person or business needs to do in order to satisfactorily complete the agreed arrangement and adding your signature to that document means you have understood and agreed to what is written in it.

The problem for you as a young adult, is that you have no experience with contracts and may quite happily sign documents you have no understanding of. The documents you are required to sign can be full of big words, confusing language and smaller print (fine print). This is designed to trap the unwary person into committing themselves to high interest rates and/or other penalties if they fail to meet the 'conditions' of the documents they signed.

This is why it is **VERY, VERY IMPORTANT** to **TAKE YOUR TIME**, do your *research* before you sign, ask questions and get any paperwork checked by someone who *IS NOT* going to benefit from the document you are signing. You also need to understand what will happen if you do not honour your commitment to the agreement. If at any stage you feel you are **UNDER PRESSURE** to **SIGN ANYTHING**, walk away and think about it.

You really *NEED* to avoid getting loans and signing Loan Agreements. If you are on a strict budget already a loan agreement is only going to trap you in the 'debt cycle'. Refer to the chapter about the 'Debt Cycle'.

You need to understand what it means to sign a written contract. It is an official document that can be legally used against you if you do not honour your commitment to the conditions you agreed to and signed.

If you miss a payment you may get phone calls to remind you, you will get threatening letters if you keep missing payments and if it continues, the item you purchased will probably be taken back and your credit rating will go down, which basically tells every business in your country that you are a risky person to lend money to or give 'credit' to.

LOAN CONTRACTS can be really bad for you

Even if the item is an investment. Before you buy anything big that is new, or for a high price, *THINK*, could something less expensive do the same job? If the answer is 'Yes' then search out that cheaper option and avoid being tied down by a Loan Agreement.

Until a contract is signed by both parties, nothing is certain

It does not matter whether it is the fall of the hammer at auction or a verbal agreement, it does not become legally official until the correct paperwork is signed. Until the paperwork is properly completed you can always back out.

Make sure you understand *EVERY* aspect of *EVERY* agreement or contract *BEFORE* you sign

Salespeople are trained to say the right things to get you to sign. Ask lots of questions and see how they respond. If you have any doubts, leave and think about it. The product is usually still available after you have sought *advice*.

To seek the answers you require, you *MUST ASK* the *RIGHT* questions

This is a skill that takes a while to get right. Take the time to think about the answer you want and construct (make/ask) the question to get that answer.

ALWAYS READ the 'Fine Print'

Every contract has big words and small writing designed to confuse you. Ask the salesperson to explain the fine print after you have read it. Never believe anyone telling you that the fine print on a document is not important. Any small printing in a document is designed for you to 'skim' over, but it usually contains 'traps' for the unwary person. It would be best if you asked for a photocopy of the document and took it home to read it. If you don't understand anything in the document you need to take it to someone who can explain it to you. Then make your decision about signing it.

BEFORE you *SIGN ANYTHING, READ* the document, *ASK* questions

Say to the person: 'Is there anything else I should know?' The person may have to, by law, tell you of your responsibilities regarding the document. It is called 'full disclosure.' If they say there is nothing else to inform you of, ask them:

> 'What are the traps of this document?'
> 'What are the penalties for missing a payment?'

When buying high priced items (house/car) sign the paperwork only *AFTER* you get quality independent legal advice and an independent valuation. Then, if there is no pressure and you are comfortable (in your mind, not your heart), complete the paperwork and get a copy. Make notes on the document (the persons name, day, time and contact number).

ALWAYS be prepared to walk away. The trap you fall into today, will probably bring you unhappiness down the track.

Once you have signed a contract, the law may allow you a period of time to back out of that contract.

This is called a **'cooling off'** period. It is a safety net for consumers when they leave the 'store' and after thinking about it, feel they have over committed themselves financially or the emotional attachment was too great to resist. Cooling off periods are usually one to five business days. You do not usually need to give a reason but a fee may be payable to the seller and they have to return your money by a certain date. **You should check consumer laws regarding 'cooling off' periods in your State /Province or Country.**

Quality, independent legal advice and independent valuation

This means you find your own professionals to do the job. Do not use the seller's professionals (finance company, lawyers) because they may benefit from you buying the product.

On *ANY* loan contract always *CHECK* the *INTEREST RATE*

Especially exactly how much you will pay over the life of any purchase agreement. Be aware large retail stores usually have a finance company that may charge very high rates of interest outside interest free periods.

Professional People

When I say professional people it means people who are trained in a specialised area to give you the right advice for your situation. Generally they will have an office where they do business and they will be dressed very well. Examples of these professional people would be lawyers, real estate agents, insurance agents, car salesmen and bankers etc.

BUT just because a professional person wears a suit, does not mean you are getting the best service or advice. In every job, there are people who are good at their job and people who are not so good at their job.

Because you are young, some people you deal with may want to take advantage of your lack of life experience, innocence and ignorance. They can do this by charging you too much money, give you bad service or give you bad advice.

What you should do is listen to your gut instinct, do your own research, get a second or third opinion but especially ***DON'T SIGN ANYTHING,*** or buy anything if you are not happy or you do not understand what they are telling you.

Do not buy during an interest free period or pay later scheme

Only make the purchase if you can afford it now. It is much better to buy something second-hand than to take out a loan agreement for something new. But if you feel ***NEED*** to sign any loan agreement please make sure you pay the item off as soon as possible otherwise the interest rate may really hurt your payments and budget. By paying later, you run the risk of your budget being too tight when your payments are due to be made. Interest free or pay-later items may have traps (late payment fees and more) for the unwary person.

Remember, when you have the amount of the item saved and the money is immediately available to you (cash/debit card) you should be able to get the price down a lot further than the ticketed price.

Retirement

YES, YOU DEFINITELY NEED TO THINK ABOUT IT

People are living much longer than they used to. You may live more than 25 years after you retire.

When there is *NO* guaranteed job for life, it is important you start saving for retirement and investing as soon as possible.

In May 2014 the Australian Government proposed in its budget to raise the retirement age to 70. Other countries may do the same to keep you working longer and paying more tax. By doing this the government saves it's money by paying out any retirement pension you may be entitled to, at a later date.

People are now choosing to have smaller families so fewer children are born. Fewer children means fewer future workers will pay taxes to pay pensions to support retiring people, if you don't provide for yourself.

For those people who get a full or partial pension, the government may no longer increase it in line with inflation therefore it will slowly lose value.

Governments of countries in future may also look at superannuation funds as a replacement for pensions except for very poor people.

NOTE: If there is no government pension or compulsory national superannuation scheme available in your country, then saving for your retirement needs to start as soon as possible.

Saving for retirement should start at around age 25. This allows time for people to complete any tertiary education and get together money for possessions such as furniture and a car. ***Even with a government superannuation scheme those payments still won't be enough for you to have a comfortable retirement.*** *You need to start saving as soon as possible.*

Refer to the chapters regarding superannuation.

DID YOU KNOW?

Up to 80% of retired people may have an income of less than $US23,000 per year. And a lot of them rely on government pensions for that amount.

A single person *TODAY* may need $25,000/year just to survive

Costs include rates, utilities (power/phone), car running costs, insurances, food, clothing etc. The amount above does not include any luxuries or holidays.

A single person may need to aim for the equivalent of $40,000/year in today's money in 50 years time

Everyone is different, but if you feel $US40,000 in today's money would provide a comfortable lifestyle in retirement, then you *NEED* to aim for the equal amount in 50 years time. Inflation means that prices may double twice (meaning your currency loses value) between 2015 and 2065.

A COUPLE retiring *TODAY* may need $35,000/year just to survive

Costs are the same as per those listed for retiring single people above.

A couple may need to aim for the equivalent of $60,000/year in today's money in 50 years time

Everyone is different, but if you feel $US60,000 in today's money would provide a comfortable lifestyle in retirement, then you *NEED* to aim for the equal amount in 50 years time.

Go online and search for 'How much money will I need in retirement'

There are many sites available that can calculate the amount needed based on the information you provide.

The family home is not necessary in retirement

The family has left. It is now too big. It swallows up a lot of your available budget in maintenance, insurance and rates per year. It may be time to move into something smaller.

Your retirement income should be made up of periods of interest or rent you receive from the investments you have made during your working life
Some investments pay out at the end of their investment period. You have the option of re-investing some or all of it, if you don't require the money.

The average household at retirement has **less than 20%** in income producing assets. Millionaire households at retirement **have at least 60%** in income producing assets.

Millionaires may also have a good portion of their wealth available in cash to buy undervalued assets from those retired people (up to 80%) that may have to sell their things to survive.

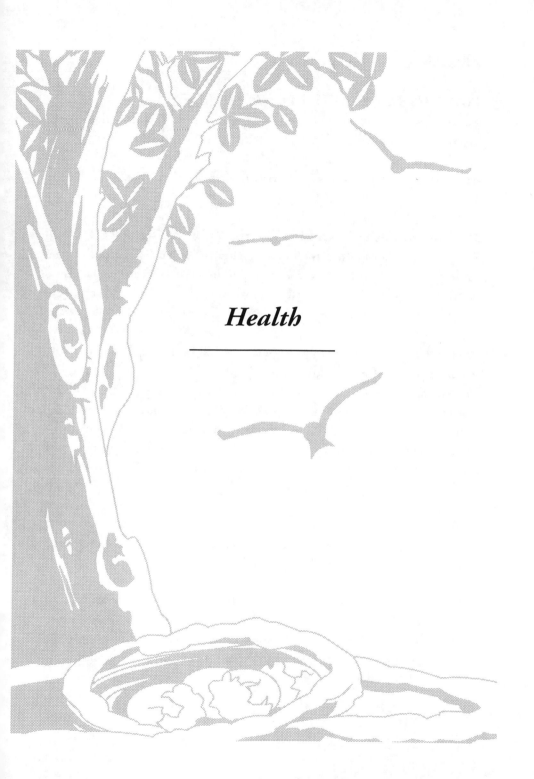

Health

Health and Lifestyle

YOU MUST LOOK AFTER YOUR HEALTH
No one else is going to. You need your health to work, earn money and survive. The better you look after yourself, the longer you may live.

Anything you do can have *bad results* for *other people.*
Think, before you act.

Most Importantly: *WASH YOUR HANDS…REGULARLY.*
This should be done at the usual times…after the toilet, before meals, after you have been out. All the surfaces that you touch have been touched by a number of people with hygiene habits far worse than your own. Paper money, your phone and computer keyboards are probably dirtier than a toilet bowl.

In an emergency, emergency services need to know vital information including your *EXACT* location.
This is information that may save your life and includes **any *MEDICATION* you are taking, any *MEDICAL CONDITIONS* you have and anything that you are allergic to.** This is especially important if you are unable to answer questions because you are unconscious (blacked out), your parents can't be contacted or there is no one around who knows you. This information needs to be available.

If you are living away from home write this information down and post it somewhere easily accessible in your living space (?kitchen) along with who to contact and their phone number (probably your parents).

If emergency medical staff do not know this information, they are limited to doing basic life support until you arrive at hospital. However if they know what you are allergic to, the medications you are taking and any medical condition you have, they can give you more effective treatment that ultimately gives you a better chance of survival.

Another thought to consider. If you are living at home, your parent(s) will know your medical information, but what do you know about *your parents'* allergies, medications, blood type and medical conditions if one of them is unconscious. The emergency services will need to know this information quickly in order to have a better chance of giving them effective treatment or even saving *their* life.

Your Medical Info in Your Phone

You always have your phone with you so why not make it a ***tool that may save your life.*** In your 'phone book' make a new contact…000 Medical Info (this will be easily visible on the first page of your contacts) and write down your blood type, medical conditions, allergies and any medication you are taking.

If you are out with friends, tell one of them the code to your phone so they can access any medical info in it if you are 'blacked out' and need emergency medical attention.

Know your way out of the house in an emergency

Have a plan to get out of the house using different exits if there is a fire. Make sure that any security screens on doors or windows can be easily removed from inside. If you are in rented premises and there is no easy exit report it to the letting agent or landlord. By law they have to ensure the premises are safe.

Be 'Sun Smart'. Slip on a shirt, Slop on sunscreen, Slap on a hat

You know the danger. Skin cancer is becoming more and more common amongst older people who did not take precautions often enough when they were younger.

Whenever you are outside you should be avoiding the sun (where possible) in the middle of the day and staying in the shade (where possible) at other times, applying 30+ SPF sunscreen every two hours, using lip balm, wearing sunglasses and a wide brimmed hat as well as drinking plenty of fluids (not alcohol) to hydrate.

Get moles and freckles checked

Visit a doctor if you notice any changes in size, colour, shape or texture. Also go to the doctor if you notice anything unusual happening to your body. The sooner you get it checked out the sooner it can be treated.

Always start your day with a good breakfast
A good healthy breakfast is the fuel your body is going to need in order for you to perform at your best early in the day.

Don't smoke
It is bad for your health, and a packet a day smoker will spend around a quarter of a million dollars over a lifetime. Yes, you read that correctly. A quarter of a million dollars.

Limit alcohol
It is about having enough to stay in control of yourself but also having a good time. It is a very, very fine line. See the chapter on Alcohol.

Exercise regularly
Exercise can take many forms. Do at least 20 minutes per day, three days per week. If, at any time in your life you haven't exercised for a while, and you want to start exercising again you should get a check up from a doctor first.

Stretch for at least 15 minutes before major exercise
Warming up the muscle groups you are about to use gets them used to the stress you are about to put on them, which may help lessen any injury to them.

Proper breathing technique
Breathe in through your nose to fully inflate the lungs and breathe out through your mouth. Breathing in through your mouth does not fully inflate the lungs. When doing exercise you need to maintain this routine…in through the nose and out through the mouth to gain full use of the lungs.

When doing exercise that involves taking the 'strain' or taking a shot such as lifting weights, rowing, shooting, tennis, basketball etc, you *DO NOT* breathe in when you are performing that move, because it places an internal strain on the body (tension) and you are not relaxed. You need to be relaxed when taking the strain or shot, so either breathe out through your mouth as you do it or perform the task between breaths.

Whenever you remember, take in three or four deep breaths
In through the nose, out through the mouth. This is done to re-vitalise your system with oxygen.

Always wash your body as soon as you can after exercise

Your sweat glands are open and need to be cleaned. Otherwise your skin is prone to clogged pores which can make it difficult for the skin to 'breathe'. You are also prone to body odour.

Get regular health checks

See your doctor at least once a year and see your dentist at least twice a year. Your diet may involve a lot of fast ('junk') food, soft drinks and processed food containing sugars and fats. Unless you change your attitude and eat healthier you will be very prone to lifestyle diseases such as Stroke and Diabetes.

EVERYTHING IN MODERATION

Regular and large amounts of smoking, alcohol, stress, and unhealthy food may lead to your body systems breaking down at some stage in your life.

Beware of a high protein diet

Your body is only able to fully digest 20 grams of protein at one time. That is why body builders eat six times a day. The danger comes from excess protein staying in your blood vessels and over time may cause a blockage leading to a heart attack. With any high protein diet, make sure you drink plenty of clear fluids (three litres per day) to flush the excess protein out of the body.

High protein foods include: red meat, fish, white meat (chicken and pork), eggs, cheese, most varieties of nuts, and of course protein shakes.

Keep your weight under control

Obesity is a leading health problem. It puts a strain on all body systems and is a major factor in Type II diabetes. Depending on a number of factors the average ideal healthy waist size throughout your life for:

> males is *LESS THAN* 92cms
> females is *LESS THAN* 80cms.

Stress

By keeping your life as simple as possible, you will cut down on a lot of stress. Excess stress may affect your health and relationships. Manage your job, time, money and relationships well.

Your body is 60-70% water and it needs to be constantly re-hydrated.
Not just in hot climates, but to also 'flush out' your system. Ideal fluids
include water, juices, tea. Alcohol, coffee or soft drinks are not good fluids to
restore your body's fluid level because they either have the opposite effect or
contain a lot of sugar and carbon dioxide.

**Carbonated drinks (soft drinks) are one of the worst substances
you can put in your body**
All that carbon dioxide and sugar is really bad for your health. You should
choose better options such as juices, cordial, water, tea or milk.

Do not work long hours for long periods
Otherwise your ability to sleep, exercise, remain healthy and keep your
relationship in good spirits will be very limited.

Back pain
About 80% of people will suffer from some sort of back complaint in their
lives. Most back problems start from back strain caused by bad posture and
the incorrect lifting of heavy objects.

Stretch your back *BEFORE* heavy lifting
Place the palms of your hand either side of your lower spine, spread your feet
shoulder width apart and arch your back gently backwards. Repeat two - three
times.

Lifting something heavy
Firstly you need to plan the lift. Know where you need to go, keep the pathway
clear and use a countdown before you lift (when using other people). When
lifting (a large box for example), get close to the object, bend down at the
knees and get a good hold of the object close to your chest. Keep your legs
shoulder width apart, your back straight, tighten your stomach muscles and
use your leg muscles to raise your body. *DO NOT* hold your breath. Most
workplaces have a limit on the weight one person can lift. Use mechanical
lifting equipment or extra people wherever possible.

Use it or lose it

In your youth, you are naturally active, but as you get older it is more difficult to find time to exercise. Your muscles get weaker and your bones aren't as flexible. Having an exercise routine three times a week, 20 minutes at a time should keep skin, muscles and bones in good healthy condition.

Exercise your brain

Regularly give yourself little projects to get through. They will take your mind away from the daily grind of life and the planning and carrying out of the project will energise your body and brain. It could be a small renovation, personal research, gardening, or your hobby etc. Also go on-line and search 'brain games'.

Exercising if you have a medical condition

You should always see a doctor before starting any form of exercise.

Five to six hours of solid sleep is much better than eight hours of dozing

If your mind is not calm and relaxed before bed, you will not get enough quality sleep.

Power napping

This is done by lying down and relaxing your body for 10 minutes *ONLY*. Five minutes is equivalent to one hour's normal sleep. Your mind is active (think about things coming up) but your body is resting. It is best to do it between 12 noon and 1.30pm. If you are having a late night, you may get a natural energy kick late in the evening that gives you a couple of extra hours waking time.

A medium to firm mattress is important for spinal health

A soft mattress does not give the spine any support.

Take an anti-oxidant supplement

'Free radicals' are rogue cells caused by lifestyle factors such as smoking, pollution, stress, alcohol and disease and may become cancerous. Anti-oxidants such Vitamins A, C, E, selenium, pine bark extract, grape seed extract and krill oil 'mop' up these rogue cells and get rid of them from the body.

Treatment for sunburn

Aloe Vera gel is best straight from the plant or a gel that contains a high percentage of Aloe Vera. A cold shower on the affected area will help ease the pain for a while. If the burn is severe, it will require the same treatment as any other serious burn. Ice (wrapped in a damp tea towel) applied to the affected area at regular intervals (usually 20 minutes) every one to two hours, for the first 24 hours following the exposure, is a very effective remedy. Seek medical assistance immediately if the skin blisters.

NOTE: Ice applied directly to the skin can cause its own 'burn'. That is why ice needs something between it and the skin; a damp tea-towel is ideal.

Your body has an inbuilt sixth sense

This is to warn you of physical danger and when things don't seem right. Adrenaline production increases. Your other senses are more sensitive. Recognise the signs and act accordingly. This will *NOT* be available if you are wearing headphones.

Experimentation is natural in your teens

But it comes with risk of injury or worse. It is always fun until someone gets hurt. Do you know how your body is going to react with alcohol, drugs, or party pills? Take responsibility with your life. Be aware of the dangers, ask questions, warn your friends, let other people go first and see the results before you try.

Guys listen up: Boredom breeds Accidents

Famous last words: "It'll be alright", "That looks easy", "If you can do it, I'm sure I can", "I know what I'm doing", "Hey guys, look at me"!

PLEASE do a First Aid course

You will have the knowledge to save a life. It may be your partner's life, a parent or your child's life. Imagine someone you love needing your help, sure you call an ambulance but in the time it takes to arrive, you will experience the longest time of your life and the most helpless feeling in the world.

Cardio-Pulmonary Resuscitation(CPR) or Heart Massage

NOTE; When doing CPR within the first four minutes of a 'cardiac arrest', the patient only has about a one in three chance of recovery. It may be their third heart attack. After four minutes, there is only a one in ten chance of recovery.

Oxygen starvation and previous medical history means the patient probably won't recover, but be satisfied that you tried and gave the patient every chance. **But even a one in ten chance means that the person you are helping could be that lucky tenth one, so you *must* give it your best go.**

If you get the chance, work with disabled children

Once you get used to their disabilities you will find warm natured, loving people who will appreciate the time you give them. They 'wear their hearts on their sleeve', but they 'forgive and forget' easily.

If you get the chance, work with the elderly

Their life stories are funny and vibrant and they love sharing their experiences. You also get a great insight into how difficult life used to be.

Learn the basics of self defence

A self defence course will help boost your confidence and self esteem. People are normally a target if they are viewed as 'weak'. Being able to fight back puts doubt into an attacker's mind and they may leave and choose an easier target. Use the minimum amount of force necessary to buy you some time and get to safety. Joining a self defence class with a friend means you can practice the 'moves' together when you are away from the class.

Find out about your family history

Talk to your parents and grandparents to see how much they know. There may be someone in your family researching previous generations of your family's bloodline. Knowing your 'family tree' can be very amusing and interesting. Go on-line and search for ancestry websites.

Spend quality time with those you care about

These are family, friends, your partner and don't forget to allow some time for yourself. This is the key to a balanced personal life.

Lifestyle Diseases

A lifestyle disease is something you may suffer from if your lifestyle is not healthy. Too much fast ('junk') food including soft drinks containing high levels of sugar, salt, preservatives and carbon dioxide are definitely not good for the body. Combining poor diet and nutrition with a lack of exercise is one of the main reasons increasing percentages of the population in 'western' societies are showing clear signs of becoming fat (obese). If you do not do anything about it, then you have a higher risk of getting the following conditions. By living a healthy and balanced lifestyle you can really reduce the risk of getting these diseases.

'STROKE' is ALWAYS a MEDICAL EMERGENCY
Whenever the signs of a Stroke are observed, call the
EMERGENCY NUMBER **in your local area**

What is a Stroke?
A 'stroke' is when an artery or blood vessel is blocked or bursts and interrupts the blood flow to or within the brain. It is a leading cause of death in many countries and is a major cause of adult disability.

The brain cells begin to die because of the lack of blood to an area of the brain, and abilities of the body such as speech, movement and memory can be lost.

DID YOU KNOW?
Stroke kills more women than breast cancer.
Stroke kills more men than prostate cancer.
One in every six people will have a stroke in their lifetime.
Stroke can affect anyone at any age.

Signs of a Stroke (Remember F.A.S.T)

Stroke usually affects one side of the body. This is a help in noticing that the person might have had a stroke. They can't do the same things with both sides of their body.

- **(F) Face**: Has the person's mouth drooped on one side? Ask them to smile.
- **(A) Arms**: Can the person raise both of their arms?
- **(S) Speech**: Is it slurred? Ask them to say their full name and address.
- **(T) Time**: *IS CRITICAL*. Phone 000 if in Australia, or 111 if in NZ.
Know your *EXACT* location. Keep a cool head. Take a couple of deep breaths and follow the directions of the emergency response person on the line.

Other Signs of Stroke

These may include unexplained sudden painful headache, problems with their balance or sudden blurred vision in one or both eyes.

Treatment

Make sure the area around the person is safe for you to work in. If they are awake keep the patient warm, in a comfortable position and tell them help is on the way.

BE AWARE the patient may go unconscious (black out) at any time. If this happens place them in the 'Recovery Position'. The Recovery Position helps to prevent unconscious people from dying because they were lying on their back and their tongue blocked their airway. Please go online and search "recovery position". You will find 'how to' videos.

DO NOT give any medications at all. *DO NOT* give anything to eat or drink.

For more information go online and search for 'the facts about Stroke'

TYPE II DIABETES

If you are diagnosed with Type II diabetes it means your blood has a high sugar (glucose) level. The lack of enough 'insulin' (an enzyme produced by the pancreas) or the body's resistance to insulin, stops glucose from being stored in the cells (to be used for energy at a later time), so it stays in the blood.

Type II diabetes is called a lifestyle disease because it is result of the high sugar content in popular processed, convenience and fast foods. People also do not take the time to exercise anywhere near as much as they used to. Work is nowhere as physical as it used to be and a lot of people's down time is spent in front of computers, phones and TV's playing games. This leads to people gaining weight, and countries all over the 'western world' are finding a large percentage of their population who are not only overweight, but fat (obese).

Your genetic make-up, a poor diet, waist measurement, lack of exercise and family history all play a part in whether you will get the disease.

DID YOU KNOW?

Up to eight out of every ten people with diabetes will die from a heart attack or stroke.

Symptoms may not occur for many years but may include:

- Bladder, kidney, skin, or other infections that occur often or are slow to heal;
- Feeling of being extremely tired (fatigue);
- Hunger;
- Increased thirst;
- Increased urine output.

The first sign of the disease may also be:

- Your vision is blurry;
- Your penis has erectile problems;
- Pain or numbness in the feet or hands.

Diabetes can be managed effectively. If you are told by a doctor you have Type II Diabetes you need to work with any health care provider to manage the condition. That means taking time to attend appointments, taking any medication as instructed and doing what they recommend. The first goal of your treatment is to lower your high blood sugar levels. Long-term goals are to prevent problems affecting the quality of your life.

The most important way to treat and manage Type II diabetes is *ACTIVITY AND NUTRITION.*

For more information go on-line and search for 'Diabetes and the name of your country'

Give Blood

It is a wonderful gift when people donate blood. It means someone else's life may be saved because of your generous donation. The reason we hear so much about people needing blood is because 'whole' blood only has a limited storage life (shelf life) of about five or six weeks and needs to be replaced. Whole blood contains red blood cells, plasma and platelets, but these can be separated which allows them to be used in different areas of medicine.

People's blood types are either A, B, AB or O, along with a positive or negative factor. Certain blood types cannot be given to people with other blood types. Any health problems with the person donating the blood, such as infection and disease can be passed to the person receiving the blood. That is why the screening, eligibility and testing procedures are so thorough.

About 450-500mls of your blood will be taken when you donate it. An average adult human has about 5.5 litres of blood, so you donate about one tenth of your blood.

In Your Country
To donate blood, go online and search 'donate blood' for more information.

DID YOU KNOW?

Around one in three people will need to be given blood or blood products in their lifetime.

To donate blood you may need to:

- have at least one form of photo ID;
- be aged between 16-70;
- weigh at least 45kgs;
- be in good health and not have a cold or flu, sore throat, cold sore, stomach bug or infection;
- have some food and three glasses of water/juice three hours before donating.

Generally you *cannot* donate blood if:

- you are unwell;
- have had a tattoo or body piercing in the last six months;
- you are pregnant or just given birth;
- you have a serious heart condition;
- you have a low level of iron.

There are many other factors why you may not be eligible to give blood. Go to the website and search 'Who can give' and find the FAQ's (frequently asked questions).

Medications

Medications are any pills, tablets, capsules, liquids, creams, and lotions that are either taken or applied to treat a condition or illness.

When you are prescribed medications by your doctor or pharmacist, the following information applies:

Take *ALL* medications as directed
This means how many pills or capsules of the medicine you take, how many times a day you take them and if you have to take the medication before, with or after food. Food is sometimes required as the medication by itself can damage the lining of the stomach. All this information is on a label the pharmacist will put on the packaging, as well as any other special instructions.

Take the full course of medication
Not just until the symptoms have disappeared. This is because the medication will continue to help reduce the issues that caused the original problem. Just because you are no longer suffering from the problem does not mean the problem has gone from your body.

If you experience problems when taking your medication
Some medications react badly with other ones. That is why your doctor needs to know all the medicines you are taking. If you are taking any medication that a doctor has given you and you have any sort of reaction to it (a rash, being sick, restricted breathing etc) then you must *STOP* taking it and go back and tell someone at the doctor's office as soon as possible. This may also mean you have an allergy to that medication.

Keep ALL medications out of reach of children
Because a lot of medicines are colourful, children will think they are lollies and will want to eat a lot of them. Obviously this can be very dangerous.

Store medicines in a cool, dark place
Heat can damage the medication and it may not work as well as it should because the 'active' ingredients have been damaged.

DO NOT drink alcohol while taking any course of medication

This is *IMPORTANT.* Alcohol can react badly with the medication, causing other health issues. Alcohol also makes the medication less effective therefore it takes longer for your medical problem to be sorted out.

DO NOT use other people's medications

Use *ONLY* medications that have been prescribed by a doctor for *YOU.* Your condition is probably different and you may be allergic to one of the other persons' medication ingredients.

Medicated creams for skin complaints

There are numerous skin complaints and everyone's body is different. Your doctor may have to prescribe different creams until you find one that is effective.

Extreme weather areas or remote settings

If you live in these areas it is a good idea to have three times your usual volume of medications in case you are 'cut off' through bad weather, or it is difficult to access medication on a regular basis.

Alcohol
(The Good, the Bad and the Ugly)

If you have *ANY* medical condition *OR* if you are taking *ANY* medication, it is advised that you see your doctor to discuss whether you should be drinking *ANY* alcohol.

Alcohol has a place in today's society. It is a part of the culture of every country in the world and has been right there with past generations as they built the history of your country.

Alcohol is all about ***DRINKING IN MODERATION***. When you have had just enough to feel relaxed that is the perfect amount because you are usually still aware of your actions, your speech, your safety and your instincts.

THE GOOD
In small to moderate amounts (one to two glasses), it can help us to relax after a stressful or busy day at work. Just ask any nurse, airline cabin crew, university student or person employed serving the public if there are times when they feel a 'drink' is necessary to help them unwind from a stressful day.

One or two glasses of *RED* wine have been shown to have great benefits to the body. French people have a diet high in saturated fat, yet they have a very low rate of heart attacks due to the properties of red wine they drink as part of their culture. Red wine contains anti-oxidants and other components from the grape skin and seeds which clean out the 'plaque' that can block arteries.

Having a social drink in the company of friends and family at a sporting fixture, the beach or cooking outdoors is a large part of many countries culture.

It takes very little alcohol to make you feel more relaxed which may mean you feel free to talk more openly and say what is on your mind. When it comes to the opposite sex, it may give you a bit more courage to say something or ask someone out.

THE BAD

We always hear more about the bad side of alcohol than the good side. This is because the bad effects of alcohol are a lot more graphic (visual) and get people's attention. People react to having too much alcohol in so many different ways. They can quietly sit in a corner and 'mellow' out, some people get really chatty, others get sleepy, some get 'flirty' and others become the life and soul of the party by singing and dancing.

The big problem is that alcohol stops you from being able to judge just how capable you are, of doing very ordinary things in the normal way. Some of the people you want to watch out for are the people who change into complete idiots. These are the ones who get so stupid they are a danger to themselves and everyone around them. They may want to destroy everything in their path, they may want to get into a vehicle and drive, they may want to fight or they are just plain rude and disrespectful to everyone else.

THE UGLY

The people you *NEED TO AVOID* are the ones who are deliberately out to cause trouble and alcohol is just the fuel they need to cross the line and put people's lives in real danger. I am particularly thinking of the act of 'King Hitting'. Technically a king hit is the attacking of an unsuspecting or distracted person in a fair fight. The term lately is being given when an **unsuspecting** 'random' person is hit in the head from the side or from behind and suffers severe injuries. A person with the intent of King Hitting someone is not looking for a fight, they are looking for a victim. These cowards then try to run from the scene before they are caught.

In addition to the above there are also the medical effects alcohol has on the body. Your body can handle a lot of abuse but frequently drinking large volumes of alcohol can lead to many health problems including cancer, stroke, heart problems, penis problems, and because all alcohol passes through it, liver problems.

DID YOU KNOW

Alcohol is a significant cause of relationship breakdowns. There may be verbal and physical abuse, money problems, a lack of quality time spent together as well as a lack of caring and feelings from the person who is 'drinking'.

Talking to drunk people

You cannot reason with someone who is under the influence of alcohol and some drugs. They do not have the power to think normally. If they are a friend or family you need to hang around to guide them to a taxi, home, or to bed. Forget anything that is said or promised. Chances are the next day, they won't remember saying it.

Tips when drinking alcohol

- Eat a good meal before alcohol. It delays the effects of the alcohol;
- Stick to one type of alcoholic drink;
- Do not mix different alcoholic drinks because it is a recipe for being unwell. (Ask any adult);
- Try to have one alcoholic drink, then a soft drink, water or juice etc to keep the body's fluid level up.

Hangovers are due to dehydration (not enough water in the body)

You *NEED TO KNOW* that **ONLY TIME** will sober a person up, not food, not coffee, not making them sick (they could choke), not activity and not a cold shower. Small amounts of water to drink are okay.

DO NOT take or give anyone *ANY* medication as it can react with the alcohol in a persons system.

When you are drunk:

- You are at risk of sexual assault.
- You are at risk of verbal and physical abuse including being 'King Hit'.
- You are at a much higher risk of being killed as a pedestrian.
- You are at risk of being robbed.
- Your 'guard' is down so there is no 'gut instinct' or sixth sense to help warn you of danger.

Guys, *never* have sex with a drunk girl

You cannot be really sure that she is OK about it, and when she is sober she might accuse you of rape. It could be extremely hard for you to prove your innocence.

Share the 'sober driver' duties with your friends

Share the occasions evenly. Everyone has a good time and most importantly everyone gets home safely.

NEVER walk anywhere alone if you have been drinking

GUYS and *GIRLS,* if you are seen to be stumbling around you are not in control of yourself and you become a target for assaults, robbery etc.

You NEED to look after your friends if they have been drinking too much

If someone in your group is drunk and you and your other friends are not ready to go home then please ring their parents to come and get them or let their parents or partner know you are sending them home in a taxi.

Be aware of the dangers of drink spiking

Do not leave your drink unattended. It is a chance for something to be added which can make you unwell and also unconscious. If you are unconscious, you have no control over what happens to you. You should probably finish your drink before going to the toilet or the dance floor and get a fresh one when you get back.

Never accept drinks from strangers

This is especially the case if the drink being offered is in an open glass like a cocktail, beer or a Vodka/ lemonade etc. It could be 'spiked'. The only way to know for sure that a drink has not been spiked, is if the drink is in a container that has not been opened or it is opened in front of you.

Never, ever, get into a vehicle...

if you know the driver is under the influence of alcohol or drugs or if they are angry or want to 'show off'. You have *NO* control over what will happen next.

Excuses and strategies you can use for not drinking
- You are the designated driver;
- You have work in the morning;
- You have to get up early for training;
- You have breakfast with the grandparents;

Tip: Carry lemonade with a piece of lemon in it and say it is vodka.

Alcohol and Drug information and help

Go on-line and search 'alcohol and drugs' in your country. There should be a number of information sites as well as an alcohol/drug hotline for your area if you feel you or someone else needs help. Many of these 'hotlines' are confidential meaning you usually do not have to give your details or the details of the person you are concerned about.

Illicit (Illegal) Drugs

The supplying AND taking of illicit drugs is ILLEGAL
Examples are heroin, cocaine, ice, meth, cannabis, and steroids.

If you have *ANY* medical condition **OR** you are taking *ANY* medication you should not even be thinking about taking illegal drugs because there is every likelihood they will make your condition worse.

You need to understand the difference between how alcohol and drugs are made.

Alcohol making (production) has many standards, regulations and laws such as health, hygiene, packaging etc. This means that approximately 99.9% of the products you drink are free from contamination.

However with the making of illegal drugs there are *NO* such regulations in place to guarantee your safety. Tablets and pills will have things added to the drug and you cannot be sure of the purity and amount of the substances in the pills. Also the place and conditions where the drug is made have *NO* health and hygiene standards.

This means that not only do you *NOT KNOW **WHAT*** is going *INTO YOUR BODY*, you do NOT KNOW *HOW* your body is *GOING TO REACT* to the drug. ***THIS IS VERY DANGEROUS.***

If you choose to supply or take illicit drugs, not only is it *STUPID* but you can also be prosecuted in court resulting in a criminal record that affects your future.

YOU HAVE BEEN WARNED... *PLEASE DON' T DO IT*

Depression and Anxiety

We all at some time feel unhappy about 'life, the universe and everything'. That's a normal part of being human. Often it's because something has gone wrong, we've had a disappointment, or a close friend or relative is seriously ill or has died. We can think of good reasons why we are unhappy. Eventually we get over it and get on with enjoying all the challenges and fun that make life interesting.

But what if the feeling of being unhappy doesn't go away? What if we aren't aware of any reason why we should be feeling down? Maybe it's because we are suffering from Depression (with a capital D), and need help. It is a true medical condition and not something to be ashamed of.

What is Depression?

Depression is when you have regular feelings of being in a 'low' state of mind and body. You are in a 'dark' place. You may feel as though there is nothing ahead for you to get excited about or there is nothing to aim for. Basically you feel there is no hope. You may have feelings of anger because your life is not working out as you had hoped and you may feel that normal day to day activities are just too much too handle. You may have little energy, not sleep well and just feel overwhelmed.

It can last from a few days to many years. It is not fully known what causes 'depression'. It is unlikely one single event causes it and is more likely a combination of personal factors and recent events. You may think being depressed is bad enough, but when you have an anxiety problem attached to it, your emotions can get out of control. It is a very common disorder among people from early teens onwards, although it can start a lot earlier.

What is Anxiety?

It is not fully understood why, but anxiety seems to be a part of most people suffering depression. Anxiety goes beyond the stress of daily life. The stress about something in your daily life goes away once the problem has been sorted out.

There are different types of anxiety including day-to-day lifestyle stresses, social fears, panic attacks, obsessive compulsive disorder's (OCD) and Post-Traumatic Stress Disorder's (PTSD).

Signs and symptoms can range from being worried a lot of the time, shaking, chest tightness, sweating a lot and dizziness through to feelings of suicide. To find out more about the signs and symptoms of anxiety disorders, go on-line and look at some websites. If you feel you are experiencing any of them and would like to talk to an experienced person about it, then phone one of the hotlines in your area.

My Own Experience

I had a bout of depression with mild anxiety for three weeks a few years ago. I had never had it before in my life. I felt there was a black cloud above me and felt there was no hope as I had nothing to aim for. I was in the middle of a bankruptcy and sat in my home office one morning thinking about my life so far.

While to some people my life would seem exciting, it had not got to where I wanted it to be. I was fortunate enough to have an emergency fund to get me out of a financial emergency if needed, but I felt my life had not moved forward for a long time. My energy level and my appetite for some reason, did not drop.

I actually had positive thoughts that I was having a bad day and tomorrow would be better. But after three weeks I had to do something. I didn't realise I was depressed so I didn't 'google' it and find the help I needed. There were thoughts of suicide and after two days of trying unsuccessfully to reach out for community assistance and failing, I decided to ring my sister. That call turned things around. It's never easy to admit you are feeling down or you have failed your own expectations, but my talking about it got me back on track. My sister said she it was something she had experienced as well. She also said she was attending a wedding in Brisbane in 6 weeks and would come and visit for a week before that. Within a day the dark cloud lifted and I had something to get excited about. Life had just got better.

Other people may not be as fortunate as I was. Their friends and family may not understand what is happening to them.

The big lesson I learned is **you have to talk to someone who understands what you are going through**.

When you ring a 'Depression' hotline there are wonderful people who know what you are feeling and are ready to listen. You don't always have to give your name (anonymous) and the person at the other end of the phone does not share any information you provide (confidential) except in exceptional circumstances.

To contact an organisation in your area

Go online and search for 'depression services' and hotlines.

I am Having a Tough Time

Good 'mental health' means you are able go through day-to-day life and you are able to cope well with juggling the pressures of work, home and social life. Your life has meaning and you have a positive attitude because you know where your life is headed and what you want to achieve. You are in a 'good place' and feel 'free'.

However, for a lot of young people, juggling the pressures of everyday life can be very difficult. Not everyone knows where their life is headed when they leave school and having a positive attitude is not easy when they find that getting a job is proving difficult. Even when a job is found, it can bring its own pressures like having a demanding boss, more work for you due to a lack of staff or you don't 'click' with the people you work with.

Any pressure at work combined with any problems at home, with transport, with a partner, finding time to pay bills, make and attend appointments, and anything else that comes up, can leave anyone with a feeling that things are getting on top of them.

If you do not take steps to get these stresses sorted out, your life will only get worse as more problems come up and you may find that you are turning to negative influences (alcohol/drugs) to relieve that pressure.

The biggest mistake people make when they have lots of stress-causing problems is thinking that they can all be solved at once. But that never works and just causes the stress to build further. What you have to do is deal with the problems *one at a time*.

These are some things you can do to relieve this stress.

- Firstly write down where the stress comes from in your life. Just by doing this you are working out where all the pressures comes from. For each one of those stresses (job, I don't have enough time, car needs fixing etc), write down what it is about those things that causes you to feel pressured.

- Tell someone; your boss, your parent(s), a trusted adult. A problem shared is a problem halved. Adult role models have a lot of experience and can offer guidance.
- Work out what the most important things are that need fixing so you can concentrate on getting those done and release some of the pressure. It may mean juggling your time by taking a day off work or study.
- A good idea is to have a plan for your day and for your week. Operate a diary for your life that allows you to write down what you need to do each day of the week. Write down any appointments, contact numbers, bills to pay etc. By doing this you become organised and break down the confusing jumble of things to do, into smaller easy-to-handle bits.
- Money pressures may be relieved by working out a budget. Finding out where your money goes and cutting back unnecessary spending gives you extra money for paying bills.

Finally if you still feel life is getting on top of you there are some very helpful government and community organisations. They receive thousands of calls a year from young people having a tough time and needing someone to listen and guide them.

To contact an organisation in your area

Go online and search for 'youth' services and hotlines.

Sexuality Confusion

As you already know, growing up through the teenage years can be a confusing time. In addition to dealing with puberty and the changes your body and mind goes through as you move into adulthood, another question arises within you... what is my sexual orientation?

Why should there be confusion? First, let's get the words right. There's 'gender' and there's 'sex" and they are used as though they are the same thing. But they're not. Gender is 'what's between your ears' and sex is 'what's between your legs'. Your brain and your body usually develop so that the gender and sex are both male or both female, but it doesn't always work out exactly like that. This can lead to confusion. Maybe your body has all of usual male bits, but your brain thinks more like a female's does. Or vice versa.

Generally our sex is pretty clear. But gender can be *almost* 100% male or *almost* 100% female *or anything in between*. That's the source of the confusion.

Even just 'random' thoughts popping into your head of intimate relations with a person of the same sex is enough to question where your sexual path is leading. You may already know whether you are definitely straight, bi-sexual, gay, lesbian etc, but there are plenty of people your age struggling to work out what their sexual identity is.

Being SSA (same-sex attracted) in today's society is normal but there is still a lot disapproval and homophobia (fear of gay people) surrounding different lifestyles, partly because of the religious based society we live in, but mainly through a lack of understanding.

For those people who are confused about their sexuality, you may need to take time and explore it further. Seek more knowledge but do it in a way that does not put your safety and feelings of comfort at risk. There may be on-line forums and gay/lesbian counselling services in your area to answer your questions.

There are usually conflicting feelings about whether or not to 'come out' and let the world know who you are. Any announcement should wait until after you have thought about a lot of things, including how you are going to deal with any discrimination or harassment that may come your way, any loss of emotional or financial support, verbal or physical abuse, gossip, and people you don't want to know, finding out. If and when you do decide to do it, the right time, as well as the person you are telling is very important. Just telling someone is going to feel 'like a weight has been lifted off your shoulders'.

Remember you are not alone. There are young people throughout your country struggling with their sexuality. It is a difficult time of your life so please contact a 'hotline' in your area because there are people who understand what you are going through and will listen and guide you.

To contact an organisation in your area

Go online and search for Gay, Lesbian or Transgender services

Stages of Grief When Dealing with Loss

Grief not only applies to death, but any form of personal loss such as your job (and income), your relationship, your health (through injury or disease) or addiction. The more the sense of loss you feel, the more heartache you tend to suffer.

We deal with losses in stages, which are most obvious in the case of death, and the descriptions below assume a death has occurred. The stages to some degree have been found to apply in all serious cases.

The stages have been identified as progressive, but because human beings are different to each other, each person deals with grief in their own way. It can take anywhere from one day to many years to fully move on from the effects of grief depending on the degree of loss to an individual. Stages may be skipped altogether or returned to later but they cannot be rushed. Only the person experiencing the grief will know when it is time to concentrate on their life again. As a friend of a grieving person all you can do is to be there to support them as best you can.

1st Stage: Shock and Denial

It is very common to react to learning of any major loss with numbed disbelief, especially if it is sudden. Shock is the body's way of providing emotional protection so that you are not overwhelmed all at once. Denying the reality of the loss is common also, as it offers protection from what has occurred. This stage may last for weeks.

2nd Stage: Pain and Guilt

As the cloud covering you in your state of shock, begins to lift, it can be replaced with unbelievable pain. It is very important that you experience this pain fully as it will allow you to move through the grief stages. Avoiding and hiding this pain or using alcohol or drugs to escape it, may just delay your journey to the place in your mind where you can function well enough to continue day to day life.

It is usual for people experiencing grief to think about what they could or should have done. This is very normal and while you may be feeling guilty about it, there is nothing that can be done to change the situation. There might be a lesson learned for the future but at present life usually just feels chaotic and a little scary.

3rd Stage: Anger and Bargaining

As the pain of the loss wears off, it may be replaced by anger and frustration. This can be the time where your mind is clear enough to find out what exactly happened or what went wrong. There may be a lot of bottled up emotions and you should find ways to release these emotions constructively. If you 'lash out' and say things that are hurtful to family and friends in your pursuit of answers, permanent damage to those relationships can occur.

You may be angry at 'the powers that be' and say 'Why me?' Bargaining is a way of deflecting the hurt you are experiencing by offering a way for you to feel better. Such statements like "I'll go to church every Sunday if you just bring them back" are common.

4th Stage: Depression (not clinical), Reflection, Loneliness

When you realise that any 'bargaining' has not worked, and your friends think you should be getting on with your life, chances are you will experience a long period of sad reflection. Although they mean well, you may just want to spend time alone and remember the good times you shared. This will cause you to realise the true magnitude of your loss and the feelings of emptiness and hopelessness in this period are common. This is a normal part of the grieving process.

5th Stage: The Upward Turn

There will come a time where you can start to adjust to life without your loved one. The reality of your loss is more accepted. Any anger has lessened dramatically and your life is becoming a little calmer and a little more organised.

6ᵗʰ Stage: Reconstruction and Working Through

As your mind becomes more functional, you are able to fend for yourself a lot more. You are able to start tackling household or day to day problems that your loved one took care of. You will start to be more social and begin rebuilding the relationships you had with friends.

7ᵗʰ Stage: Acceptance and Hope

Acceptance of a major loss is never easy. It does not mean instant happiness and while you will never return to the person you were before this life changing event, there is enough 'hope' in your future to go forward. You are able to actively plan things and function much better. The turmoil of your loss is behind you and while you often think about your loved one, much of the pain has gone. Hopefully you will once again look forward to some good times to come, and find joy again in the experience of living.

For information on how to deal with grief, go on line and search 'grief counselling'

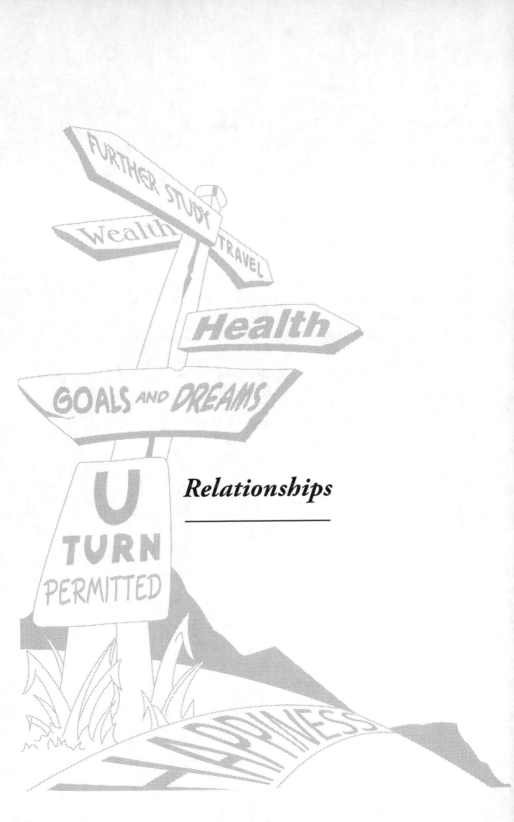

Relationships

Relationships
(The *GOOD*, the *BAD* and the *UGLY* Signs)

You will find out fairly quickly (if not already) that really good relationships are hard to find. This is because everyone is so different. They think differently as well as having different values and goals. Perhaps the hardest lesson that can take a lifetime to learn is how to recognise your partners true feelings for you. That's because men and women have quite different ideas of what 'love' is and how to show it. For most of us it takes a lot of time and lots of experience before we are able to understand and live with the differences.

Confusing Love and Sex
Making love is when the body and mind of both people are physically and spiritually absorbed in each other. However, this connection usually only develops after a period of time and 'dating' (the time depends on the couple) when you are finding out about each other. Finding your 'soul mate' may take a while and until that happens there may be instances where you get to have sex, but unless there are genuine feelings of 'being in love' from *BOTH* people you will need to continue your quest for true love.

Signs of a Good Relationship
Being in a healthy relationship is a great feeling. You feel as though you are both on the same wavelength and you have a good idea what you both want out of life. You have more than a friendship, possibly a soul mate, not just a relationship based on sex.

You like doing things for your partner and it makes you feel really good when they smile because of your efforts. You feel safe with your partner. You have fun together but you also spend time away from each other doing your own thing. Your secrets are safe and you feel you can talk to your partner without being judged. There is no pressure from your partner to be anything other than who you are.

Mutual trust and respect are the main ingredients for any relationship but good communication is essential. Communication means actually listening to what the other person is saying and when you do not agree on something, you both try and work it out in a calm manner by reaching a solution you can both live with. Of course, this is much easier said than done, and if it doesn't work all of the time it doesn't mean that you are headed for the end of your relationship.

Signs of a Bad Relationship
The signs of a bad relationship are when the things that make up a good relationship are not happening. There is little trust or respect, disagreements turn into arguments regularly, you do not smile much, you are expected to do things to please your partner, there is little expression of love or passion, you are being judged constantly and you can't relax or be yourself.

You should seriously think about ending your relationship if the following occur often:
- your thoughts, views and ideas (opinions) are not considered;
- you feel pressured to do anything you don't want to do;
- you're told what to wear;
- you get 'put down' regularly;
- you are hit or threatened and/or you are expected to lie;
- you constantly 'give' to the relationship and get nothing in return;
- you are cheated on (once may be enough).

For more information or assistance in your country, go on-line and search 'relationship problems'. There will be websites with hotlines that can help.

The 'UGLY' part of relationships is covered in the *NEXT* chapter… Domestic Violence

Domestic Violence
(the *UGLY* side of relationships)

The law, in your country may regard domestic violence as actual or threats of assault including sexual assault, personal injury and intimidation, between partners, spouses, de factos and family members. Note that word "intimidation" - you don't have to have bruises and black eyes, the fear of getting them may be enough.

If you are a *VICTIM* of Domestic Violence.
This is all about *YOUR SAFETY*

If you are in *IMMEDIATE DANGER*
Call the *EMERGENCY NUMBER* in your country

> If there is no immediate danger, call a domestic violence hotline'. They will listen, understand and advise you about what you can do. Go online and search for 'domestic violence hotline' and the name of your country. There should be many services available, usually free and confidential.

Signs of an Ugly Relationship

If you are physically and/or verbally abused by a partner
Ask yourself, "Is it a one-off incident or it has been getting worse over time"?

If it has been getting worse, or happening more often, you should tell someone you trust (family or friends) what has been happening and by taking that brave step you will hopefully feel that a weight has been lifted off your shoulders. Just by telling someone you have a domestic violence problem in your life now means you have admitted it and you can work out what the next step should be. It may be another decision whether or not to report it to police.

If you do report it to the police, you are creating a 'paper trail' and a history that will be taken into account if it happens again. However in some regions the police do not like to get involved unless there has been obvious injury or damage. Talk to a hotline first, and you may be advised to involve the police.

If the abuse (physical/verbal) has been happening often you may want to try and talk to the abuser when they are in a 'sober' and relaxed mood about their actions and why they feel there is a need to treat you the way they do.

Being around an abusive partner is only going to break down your feelings of self worth. The lack of self worth (self esteem) is a downward spiral to depression. You need to get help as soon as possible. Call a hotline.

It is easy for people to say you need to leave, but actually doing it can be difficult due to many other circumstances. You may feel trapped because you have no access to money, or you don't know of anywhere else to go. Or you might feel ashamed that your relationship has broken down and you don't want to be told "I told you so" by friends who warned you about your partner. Maybe you just hope that your partner will be better in future. You need to talk to people (a professional, a hotline, friends or family) to help you be realistic about your circumstances and work out what is best for you to do.

Domestic violence against you is in no way a failure on your part. It is your partner expressing their feelings in the wrong way.

GUYS...LISTEN UP: *DOMESTIC VIOLENCE HAPPENS TO MALES AS WELL*

It happens more than people realise. A lot of home violence towards males goes unreported because of the embarrassment a male may have admitting that it is happening. If you are being physically or verbally abused by your partner you need to report it but you need to prove you are the victim. Because male victims are less common, people may be less serious about believing you.

To give you an example… neighbours call the police and they come to your place but your partner says *they* are the victim and you say you are the victim. Who do you think the police are going to believe? You are going to need proof, voice recordings, mobile phone camera, neighbours as witnesses, and previous complaints to police etc.

As mentioned above, leaving may be difficult due to a variety of reasons. Ideally you need to be somewhere you are safe so you can think clearly and work out the best course of action to take. A trusted friend by your side to offer support, help and advice is a good thing because they can see your problem from a clear point of view. If you feel you are alone with this problem please call a Domestic Violence hotline in your area because they can generally offer you clear options to help your immediate future.

For Girls

Life will present you with many unexpected challenges. The following tips and information should help you as you move forward into one of the most exciting phases of your life.

RESPECT YOURSELF
If you do not show any respect for yourself, no-one else will. Dress appropriately. Be polite and respectful to other people.

Beware of sexting
A picture lives forever… *FOREVER.* You will have no control over who views any naked or revealing pictures of yourself that you send via social media, and where they end up. People you meet who have seen them may form the wrong opinion of you and it could cost you the career or opportunity you wanted.

Actresses and Super-models
They are human just like you, only they have to look really good to do their job. They have a team of professionals covering up every flaw and using every trick in the make-up and fashion industry to make them look perfect. Grab any women's magazine and look for celebrities out and about on their days off. You are probably looking better than they are.

Listen to your 'gut' instinct
It gives you a sense of what is good and bad.

Never let anyone try to change who you are
You are unique and special in your own right. Maybe there are some areas you want to improve on and you should do some research and make a decision based on that research, if you feel improvement is necessary.

Trust your mother's (or your female role model's) advice
She has probably been there, and had to deal with it…maybe more than once.

Always keep open lines of communication with the adult role model(s) in your life

They offer support, guidance and experience when things may not be so clear to you.

Eat well

A balanced diet should include fruits, vegetables and plenty of water and juice to hydrate the body. Cut down on the junk food.

Exercise

Ensure you undertake 20 minutes at least three times a week. Walk, cycle, run, play sports. It gives you the naturally occurring 'happy chemicals' (endorphins).

Know your skin type

Talk to professional people in department stores or chemists who may be able to determine your skin type. It is important that you get the right make up for your skin.

Learn how to bring out your *BEST* features

Do your own research or talk to knowledgeable store people on how to maximise your best features and minimise your lesser features.

NOW is the time to protect your skin for the future

Use a combination of high SPF (sun protection factor) sunscreen, moisturiser and anti-wrinkle creams. Apply to face, hands and neck.

Skin Care

Every morning and night cleanse, tone, serum, moisturise. Try a moisturiser that contains anti-oxidant properties such as grape seed, vitamins A and E, kiwifruit, as well as cooling properties such as cucumber and Aloe Vera. Apply moisturiser on damp, not wet skin.

Do not wear make-up to bed

It prevents the skin from 'breathing' in order to repair itself.

Make-up tip
Use product sales assistant's at chemists and department stores to show you how to apply make-up correctly, to get the 'look' you want or basic daily routine.

Get a haircut every six to eight weeks
This routine will keep styles tidy and the ends of the hair strong. Ask the stylist for tips on the best care for your type of hair.

Do not brush wet hair
It splits the ends. Use a wide toothed comb instead.

PAP Smears (research it if you don't know)
These should be done every year if you have more than one sexual partner.

Examine your breasts
Find out how to do your own breast examination. Talk to your medical professional or go on-line and search 'Step by Step breast self examination' and select from the many sites available. Note any changes in your breasts and report them to your doctor.

Where possible keep a 'girly' pack with you
In the car or in your handbag, it might contain:, wipes, lip gloss, disinfectant gel, comb, spare cash and anything else you think you might need.

Condoms are only 97% effective when new
There is a 3% chance they won't work. Heat, exposure to sunlight and past expiry date will also make condoms even less reliable once they come out of the box.

Be aware of sexually transmitted diseases
Let's face it, most guys will say anything to get you to have sex! If you give in to his charm that's fine, but be aware you do not know his sexual history and you are taking a big risk of catching a sexually transmitted disease (STD), if you do not insist he wears a condom. There is nothing wrong with you having your own supply.

Dress for the occasion

Think what everyone else will be wearing and dress to that standard. Learn what works best for you.

Buy clothes to mix and match your wardrobe

Whether it is an item from an 'op' shop or a designer label, it is estimated that women only use 30% of the clothes in their wardrobes. Buying something that goes with a number of clothes you already have means you are likely to wear it more often.

Buying shoes

Don't just try on one shoe as most people have one foot slightly bigger than the other. Wear both shoes and walk around a little to see if they are comfortable.

Buying jeans and trousers

Make sure you sit down in them and bend over to see if they are comfortable.

Tight fitting skirts

You will develop 'panty lines' if you use your usual size underwear. A larger size underwear is recommended.

Have a bra fitting done by a specialist

80% of women do not wear the correct sized bra. Sales assistants in the bigger department stores are specifically trained in fitting you with your correct lingerie with little or no additional cost to the purchase price.

10 WARDROBE ESSENTIALS EVERY WOMAN SHOULD OWN

Nude coloured and black plain underwear

It will go well under all clothing.

A great pair of dark blue jeans

But get the right style for your shape.

A jacket or coat

Longer styles go with most outfits. Shorter styles can look more casual. Decide which style will work best with other items in your wardrobe.

Ankle boots
The right pair can go with almost any outfit and will make your legs appear longer and leaner at the same time.

A classic heel
This can range from a classic court shoe to a pair of simple strappy sandals.

A knit sweater
One that is pure wool, a neutral colour and classic style.

A little black dress
Buy a style that suits your shape. Those with darker complexions should go for dark blue or red instead.

Colourful scarf(ves)
Brighten any outfit with a soft, drapey fabric such as silk or cotton to easily transition from summer to winter.

A tailored suit
A navy or black jacket and skirt/pants will go with other wardrobe items.

Occasional day dress
Something bright and colourful in your wardrobe for the perfect 'occasion' outfit
Lisa Lyford, 'Gorgeous Me'

Boys
They think and act differently. They don't tend to show their feelings. They don't always think with their brain.

Your biggest challenge with any male
How do you know if the guy who is buying you drinks, complimenting the hell out of you and building your self-esteem, is genuinely interested in a relationship or just a one night stand? If it is a short term relationship you are after and he is hitting the right 'buttons' then you may decide to go for it, but do it safely. However, if you are looking for something more long term, keep him talking and you or your friends may soon know whether he is 'full of it' or he is actually 'for real' (genuine).

Blind dates

It is all about your safety. Give the name, location and other details of the guy you are meeting to someone else. Ideally a friend should go with you, get introduced and they can always leave if the date is going well.

When you are drunk

You are at risk of:

- sexual assault
- being robbed
- verbal and physical abuse
- being killed as a pedestrian.

Your guard is down so there is no 'gut instinct' or sixth sense to help you.

Excuses and strategies you can use for not drinking:

- you are the designated driver;
- you have work in the morning;
- you have to get up early for training;
- you have breakfast with the grandparents;
- carry a lemonade with a piece of lemon in it and say it is vodka.

Share the 'sober driver' duties with your friends

Share the occasions evenly. Everyone has a good time and most importantly, everyone gets home safely.

For Guys

That today's society is no longer tolerating bad, aggressive or stupid behaviour. *You need to 'think before you act'.* Your decisions can affect the lives of other people. Being drunk or 'out of it' is *NO LONGER* an excuse.

It's tough being a guy. Sexual prowess is a big part of your genetic make up and there is a lot of competition out there from other males looking to either 'hook up' with, or establish a relationship with a female. Each female is different from every other one and that is something you really need to understand. There will be some things the same, but what works for a girl you have been with, probably won't work for the next girl you are with.

Learn to be confident about your abilities and feel good about yourself
No one is perfect. Each person has habits, quirks or emotional 'hang ups' under the surface. The important thing to remember is to work with what you have. Focus on your good points and through your life, if you feel you need to, sort out the not so good points by seeking help.

Being yourself (being genuine) is a must
Girls generally can tell if a guy is genuine. If she doesn't pick up any 'shit' you are spinning, believe me her friends will, and they will tell her if you are 'full of it.'

Do not let your heart rule your head
This not only applies when being around girls but to any situation where your emotions can over-ride your better judgement and it ends up costing you time, money or emotional baggage. Hit your pause button and say to yourself "Do I need *REALLY* need this?"

There is a life partner out there for everyone
You just have to be in the same place at the same time to get started.

Dress up

Always try to look your best for an occasion. Blend in with the crowd but highlight your best features.

You only get one chance to make a good first impression

If you know it's coming, plan for it. Be yourself. Be confident but not 'cocky'. If she likes you even though your first impression wasn't great, she will probably give you a second or third chance.

Women need to be made to feel worth something

It's not always about the amount of money you spend (most guys will do that), but what really attracts a girl's attention is the amount of time and planning you did to make an occasion special. That, guys, earns you the *BIG* points. Showing you care and that you took the time to do it. If that doesn't work then she probably is not into you. You might want to move on *BUT* she *WILL* tell her friends what you did and it will be something she always remembers.

Communication with a girl

Talking to a girl about something you have in common is going to get you a lot further that any 'cheesy' pick up line. Humour used in the right way is a great way to start a conversation.

Don't take yourself too seriously

Learn to relax around women. Learn to laugh at yourself. If you can't laugh at yourself, who can you laugh at?

When around females, show confidence and be yourself

Most women appreciate a sense of humour. Dress well, be polite and respectful.

Hooking up with a girl is all about mutual attraction

If she doesn't like you, it isn't happening.

Talking to a 'hot' girl

Every male knows talking to a beautiful girl is a nerve wracking experience. Have a few questions for her and feed off her answers for more questions to keep the conversation flowing. You need to find out more about her interests and things you have in common in order to take any conversation with her further. Ask her opinion about different things and listen, listen, listen to what she says.

You need to know that EVERY woman is different
You will only get to know her well through regular contact. When it comes to sex, read the heading. You will only learn through practice…but the practice is awesome.

Always be prepared to wear a condom
You do not know her sexual history and she does not know yours. You don't want an embarrassing trip to the doctor's. Don't be surprised if she has her own supply. Use any 'fun' ones such as ribbed, flavoured, glow in the dark etc.

Condoms are only 97% effective when new
There is a 3% chance they won't work. Heat, exposure to sunlight and past expiry date, will all make the condom less reliable once they come out of the box.

Your *FIRST SEXUAL EXPERIENCE* will usually be a disaster
No matter what you do, you will be really nervous and critical of yourself afterward. It has happened to every male before you but it gets much better.

Never have sex with a drunk girl
You cannot be really sure that she is OK about it, and when she is sober she might accuse you of rape. It could be extremely hard for you to prove your innocence.

Never under-estimate your past history with an ex-partner
If the breakup was good, there can be benefits down the track. However, if the breakup was bad and you see her out somewhere, it might not work out so well.

Guys, take the time to listen to what your girlfriend is saying
Be sensitive to her emotional needs. One word answers are not appropriate. Offer your thoughts, suggest options but let her make the final decisions.

The dreaded 'friend' zone!!
You think she is 'smoking hot' but she has made it clear she doesn't think of you that way. "You're just a good friend." This is going to be hard to accept and very, very rarely does it change. If this situation is not acceptable, move on and direct your energy elsewhere.

Appreciate your partner

It can be as simple as saying thank you, to something on a deeper level. Be grateful for your partners efforts and be supportive of what they do.

Balance time together with doing your own thing

You need space from each other regularly to see friends or family and do things that interest you.

By being silly together it creates closeness

A pillow fight, funny voices, costume parties, tickling. Mix it up.

Never go to bed being angry at your partner

Try and work things out as best you can before going to bed, even if it means you agree to make time to discuss the issues the next day because you will both need to have quality sleep. Obviously arguing in bed is not good for the relationship either as the male will usually always end up sleeping somewhere else.

You must take emotion out of any argument

This is very hard to do because the passion behind your point of view is so powerful. The discussion has to be done when voices are calm and emotions are in check. Yelling and screaming means there is frustration at not being listened to. Once you have discussed the issue(s) causing problems, you can work towards a solution that both of you can live with.

Four aspects of a successful relationship:

- honesty; about your needs and feelings;
- communication; a willingness to open up, talk and listen;
- negotiation; you will not always agree. Find a solution both of you accept;
- trust; is the base of a strong relationship.

A successful solution is one that each person agrees on

If one person has gained more than the other, there may be feelings of resentment and may cause a relationship to break down.

Happy partner: Happy life

If your partner is not happy, you will soon know about it. Partnerships have a foundation of mutual love and respect but good communication is essential. Have your own opinions but listen to their side and find common ground.

Your Parents

Ever heard of a 'generational divide'? It's an 'official' term for the differences between generations – your generation, your parents' generation, your grandparents' generation. It's a neat way of referring to all of the differences in activities, values and goals of people of different age groups without having to spell them out.

Think of all of the generational differences between you and your parents. When they were your age there were no mobile phones and no Internet. Think about what difference that would have made to how they spent their time, how they mixed with their friends and so on. Do the same exercise with your grandparents. They not only did not have mobile phones, very few of them would have had any sort of phone when they were young.

It can be difficult for people across generational divides to understand each other. Because everyone gets so caught up with the hectic nature of their own lives it is very easy not to have enough time to see your parents or adult role model. Until you leave home your reliance on your parents is quite strong but that will lessen rapidly as you start going it alone. As you become more self sufficient and your social life increases, your visits to see your parents will become less and less.

Here's a question for you: how often do your parent(s) see their parents? It could be three times a week, although I am thinking with most parents it is more like three times a month, even if they live in the same area. The reason for this is simple... again it is the generational divide and, as mentioned above, everyone's lives become very busy. Your parent(s) have their children to worry about (you), go to work each day, maintain a relationship with their partner, have appointments, meetings and volunteer groups to attend.

Many elderly people, like your grandparents, in today's society are being ignored by their own family, because each member of that family is so caught up in their own life. What is also happening is that women are outliving their husbands by a good number of years and there are a lot of elderly women living in their own home, who have poor quality of life because they have little or no social contact.

Another area of concern contributing to the loneliness of elderly people is the breakdown of the family unit. Families have to move to other cities to get work, divorces and separations split families which can impact on the care and attention given to the elderly relations.

There are some excellent government, private and Christian nursing and home-help services in the community, but they have limited funding, staff and time resources to be able to help everyone.

You owe just about everything to your parents. You probably don't agree with everything they do and believe in, but they believed in you enough to look after you. They gave up a lot to bring you up so you could have the quality of life you have now.

They will always be concerned for you, even if they don't show it. They are probably your best and most loyal friends as well as your parents, and that still will be true as they (and you) age. So please, as they get older, make the time to be sure they are getting the quality of life they deserve. **You are going to expect the same from your kids.**

Travel

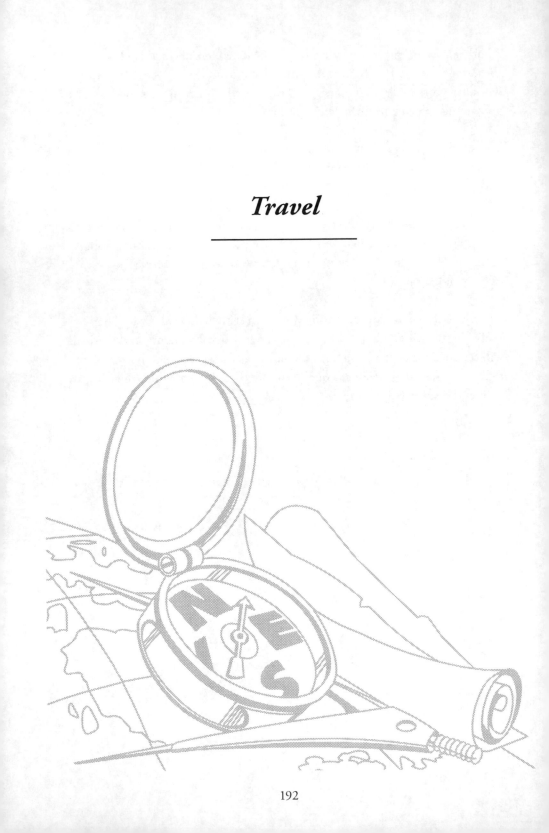

Travel

You've decided you need a break from your usual day to day life and hopefully you have saved all of your money in order to afford it. Going on holiday is a great feeling no matter how long you go for or what the purpose of your journey is. You get to see new places, experience the culture and meet new people. Like any new thing you want to do, there are plans you need to make to ensure your trip is enjoyable and safe.

Do you really want to be paying off a holiday six months after you have had it?

Have the holiday only after you have saved all or most of the money. Think how much more you are going to enjoy the holiday when you have worked and saved hard for it.

WARNING, WARNING, WARNING

If you are on public transport *ESPECIALLY* a plane and you mention any of the following words...***BOMB, EXPLOSIVES, TERRORIST*** etc, even if you are joking, you can be arrested. With the terrorism threat all around the world, small casual remarks can be taken very very seriously.

See and know about as much of your own country before going overseas

People you meet in other countries will want to know general information about your country and they might get a wrong impression because of your lack of knowledge.

Safety in numbers

Try and travel with a friend(s) and remain alert at all times. Alone you are an obvious target for scams, violence and misfortune. Thieves are experts at studying body language and your innocence will give you away immediately.

Research where you are going on an overseas holiday

Read travel guides and find out about any travel risks with the countries you plan to travel to including those covered in the latest government travel advisories. You should also find out about any local customs and if tipping for services is required.

Check out health issues you might need to consider

If you are planning to visit African, Asian or South American countries, check with your doctor at least 12 weeks before travel to see if you require vaccinations and/or anti-malarial medication etc.

Try to speak some basic words of the country's language

The fact that you are trying, means the local population may be more willing to help you. Never assume that *somebody* will understand English.

Take advantage of friends or family in places you want to visit

You can use their place as a base on holiday, or until you get established with work and accommodation.

Travelling is not relaxing

You have to confirm tickets, possibly change currencies, confirm transport and hotels or other accommodation, get past language barriers, keep a look out for danger, worry about your travel partner, organise clothing and what else you will need, cope with breakdowns and delays as well as a host of other issues.

Register with your country's foreign affairs department

Your governments 'foreign affairs' department may have a website where you can register your holiday. The information you provide may help to locate you in case of an emergency overseas, or advise you about an emergency at home.

Advise family and friends of your travel plans

Make copies of your passport, insurance policy, ticket details and 24 hour emergency numbers. Having them signed as copies of the original documents by a Justice of the Peace or Notary Public/Official will add more credibility to them. Carry one set separately from the originals and leave another set with family or friends, as they can use the information to help you from home if you lose your paperwork.

Always get an appropriate level of travel insurance

Insurance is advised for all international trips and especially important if you plan to visit certain countries (USA, Asia, South America, Africa Europe) that do not have health/medical agreements with your own country.

Travel insurance can be applied for online or at a travel agents when you book your trip. You need to have enough insurance cover to get you home if an emergency medical situation comes up. You also need to cover any planned activities that are dangerous (scuba diving, skiing), flight cancellations, delays, accommodation problems and lost luggage.

Pack one third of the clothes you think you will need

Choose your clothes for temperature ranges at that time of year. Balance casual and dress footwear. Mix and match outfits. Remember you may have to carry the weight you have packed up stairs where there are no lifts. An idea is to buy second hand clothes in charity shops when you arrive, then sell them or give them away when you leave to come home.

Reduce the amount of space your clothes take up

Roll your clothes up or use vacuum sealed bags to really shrink down the bulkiness of your clothes. Remember you may have to carry over long distances what you have packed.

You are usually allowed a 7kg 'carry on 'luggage limit

Get a flexible bag to carry in the aircraft cabin and include in your hand luggage items, pants, top, warm clothing, a change of underwear, covered footwear and basic toiletries. If your main luggage goes missing or is delayed at least you have some basic essentials to get you through.

CHECK YOUR LUGGAGE YOURSELF

This is hugely important. One of the first questions Customs officials ask is, "Did you pack your bag yourself?" Pack your bag(s) yourself and lock it securely. Every time you take it off an airport luggage 'carousel', check the lock for signs of tampering. You should open your bag and inspect it. Is it the way you packed it? Search through your belongings thoroughly for packages you don't recognise. It will be too late if Customs pick you up for unusual items during baggage x-ray.

Take a mixture of money with you

Don't rely on a single form of currency. Take a balance of travellers cheques, loaded travel cards, and cash. Allow enough to cover emergencies. Do not keep all your money in one place.

Use the office safe at your accommodation (if you think it is safe to do so) to keep your valuables secure. Divide and put your money in three different places on your body.

Limit your alcohol intake on a flight
Alcohol affects you much quicker when flying and you may be refused entry to a country if you are considered drunk.

Contact home if you are near a major disaster or incident
Your family will be worried whether are safe, so reassure them.

Know where your nearest embassy is located
In the case of a lost passport or you need 'consular' assistance.

Do not drink the local 'tap' water
When visiting countries not as 'clean' as your own, you should always use bottled water and when buying drinks they should be opened in front of you so you can see that they are fresh. Even so, you need to check the bottom of the bottle to make sure there are no needle size marks which will indicate tampering. You also need to wash all raw fruit and vegetables (in boiled, safe water) before eating them.

Just when you think it's safe ordering a drink from a bar, remember you have no idea how, or what with, those ice cubes in your drink may have been prepared. Ice cubes are enough to cause a very 'upset' stomach.

So is the water you brush your teeth in – be very careful of *ALL* water usage.

Obey local laws
The first law you come across will be sign posted all through the airport telling you what is not allowed to be brought *INTO* that particular country. Dump anything like fruit and food from the plane. Your country's government cannot intervene in other countries court processes. Being a citizen of your country does not usually entitle you to any special treatment.

Safeguard your passport at all times

Scan the details of your travel documents onto a USB memory stick. It can be difficult to replace your passport while overseas. Ensure it remains valid for at least three months after your travel ends. More information regarding lost or stolen passports can be found on-line by searching 'passports' and the name of your country.

For long trips frequently spend three days in the same place

This provides a chance to relax and refresh your mind and body and plan or think about the next leg of your journey.

Go through the 'Items to Declare' section at Customs

When exiting the baggage carousel at an airport, you should look at going through the 'Items to Declare' (RED) section as the line is usually always shorter. Declare a bag of sweets. They may look at you oddly, but you are never going to see them again and are out in the arrival's areas quickly.

Be cautious in countries you don't know

By using your 'common sense', gut instinct and sixth sense you should get through a trip without too many hassles. Travelling alone is not advisable unless you are experienced. As soon as alcohol enters the equation, things can change rapidly. There is safety in numbers and look out for each other.

Be aware of the wildlife and marine life of the places you visit

Tropical environments have 'nasties' that hide in the shallow water and can be extremely dangerous to humans. Never run into the water. Walk in and shuffle your feet to disturb any potentially harmful marine life (stone fish etc) near by and allow them to escape. *DO NOT* pick up the beautiful cone shells in the water or on the beach as the marine organism inside has a poisonous 'barb' that shoots out and is generally very toxic.

Work out what have to *DECLARE* to *CUSTOMS OFFICIALS*

When filling in Customs declarations, *READ* the brochure so you know what you have to declare and exactly the types of products you are not allowed to take into the country. If you are *NOT SURE, DECLARE IT.*

In another country you can do things outside your comfort zone

Haggle in local markets if you haven't done it before. Offer 25% of the price and don't go above 50%. You will feel a little nervous but you are on holiday. When applying for a job, don't wait for the company to contact you. Ask the interviewer what your chances are of getting the job. If they are not good, move on and focus on the next interview rather than leave, go 'home' and anxiously wait and hope for a reply.

If you buy a vehicle in another country

Make sure parts for it are available in the countries you are visiting. A classic mistake that travellers have made is the 'It will be alright' attitude and often it is not. It may add to the adventure, but why not save yourself the hassle and get an inspection done before you leave, fix the problems and take some basic parts with you.

International fast food restaurant toilets

When we weren't staying in camping grounds around Europe, a lot of our daily washing and hygiene was done in international fast food restaurant toilets. No matter what country you are in, the cleanliness of an international fast food restaurant has to meet certain standards. Otherwise be prepared to have loose coins in the currency of the country you are in. France for example, you need to pay for the use of a public toilet.

Travel Luggage

Make sure you have a contact number on your luggage when travelling. Just have the *current* labels on your luggage. Remove all other labels when starting a new leg of your journey. The old ones can cause confusion to baggage handlers and your luggage may go back to a previous destination.

For further information on travelling overseas: go online and find websites to give you other tips and information.

Things Are Not as They Seem

Challenging the 'Status Quo'

Status quo is a latin term which means the 'existing state of affairs'. Put simpler, how things are done at the moment.

We are brought up in a society that has laws, regulations and rules to keep people from causing harm to other people, property and the environment. We are taught to respect those people who make those laws (government and local authorities) and those who enforce the law (police).

So what happens when the laws that governments and local authorities make are thrown aside, regardless of people's rights, for the sake of their own big profits. What can you do when local authorities, the police and transport departments become so focused on gathering as much money as they can from people who have caused *NO* injury to anyone, *NO* damage to any property and *NO* harm to the environment?

One of the main messages that need to get out to young adults, is the need to think for themselves and to question any ideas and things that are told or shown to them because:

> that's how breakthroughs are made and
> it will serve them well throughout their lives.

You need to ask your teachers, your future bosses and those exercising any sort of "power" or "control" over you – eg police, politicians, doctors, lawyers etc, for some kind of proof of the points they are making. Then, if something doesn't "add up" or make sense, you should challenge that idea or concept further and demand some kind of additional proof. If you still are not satisfied, you should reject their claim, do your own research and find your own way forward.

As you will have found in this book, I am passionate about seeking knowledge on how things are done in 'normal', everyday life. What seems like a good method or idea may actually be designed to trick you into taking the easy way out and parting you from your money. Look at the chapter about 'Cashback' schemes, research the bad side of auctions, and please understand you are a 'free' person.

Remember you do not have to accept anything you are told, shown or is written down, without clear proof it is actually true.

'Cashback' Schemes

'Cashbacks' are an advertising tool used by the maker of a product to boost their sales and is a classic example of something not being as simple as it may seem.

The idea behind the 'cashback' scheme is that a person goes to a store and buys a product that is part of the 'cashback' promotion. They pay *FULL PRICE* for the product and then make a claim to the maker of the product or some other organisation to get a part refund of the price they paid.

The simple question you are asking yourself is 'Why doesn't the store just offer a discount on the item?'

The answer is...With a 'cashback' promotion the maker of the product can save a lot of money. Here's how they do that.

Say a $1000 computer was part of a 'normal' sale in a store with $150 off the price. Everyone who bought that computer would get it for $850. If 1000 computers were sold, the maker of the computer and the store lose 1000 X $150 = $150 000 of profit.

However, if the same $1000 computer was advertised with a $150 'cashback', the 'deal' still gets people to go to the store but after they have paid *FULL PRICE* ($1000) it is now up to them to claim the 'cashback' offered.

Firstly there is a limited time period in which to make a claim. Claiming the 'cashback' may be time consuming. Time which many people don't have. There will be a strict range of terms and conditions that people wanting the discount need to follow. They also need to access the web site, fill in all the required sections as well as provide their voucher, bar code or receipt details, which may also have to be posted to the organisation.

Some valid claims may get turned down and the small amount of people that see their claim through may not see any refund for six - twelve weeks.

Out of the 1000 people that bought the same computer on the 'cashback' scheme, maybe less than 200 will have done all the necessary steps to claim back the $150 which equals $30 000.

By advertising the computer as a 'cashback', the store got a similar amount of people to go there and buy the product at *FULL PRICE,* but the store and the maker saved $120 000 more than if they had done a basic $150 discount.

By making the refund process time consuming with tricky terms and conditions, stores can still increase sales and make good profits.

THIS IS A GOOD EXAMPLE of why you should ask questions and find out from people (in this case store salespeople) exactly what is involved before you spend your money.

There is no harm asking for the discount to be given to you in the store. If they say 'No', I would go somewhere else. They obviously are more focused on the profit than you the customer.

For further information go on-line and search 'cashback offers'.

The Top Tips

The Top Tips you need to remember

If you can do the following you should have a great life.

TREAT PEOPLE HOW YOU WANT TO BE TREATED
With politeness and respect! If you treat people badly, then expect the same in return.

IF YOU FAIL TO PREPARE (PLAN)…THEN PREPARE TO FAIL.
If you don't prepare properly when dealing with money, contracts, any sort of application, job interviews, dangerous situations, weather events etc, then you should expect a result that is not in your favour.

THINK BEFORE YOU ACT (Your Pause Button)
Thinking a bit more about anything *BEFORE* you do it can prevent mistakes and injury and save you time and money.

ALWAYS THINK ABOUT SAFETY
If you are injured, how do you earn enough money to support your lifestyle.

YOU NEED TO START AT THE BOTTOM
Your parents have nice things now because they started at the bottom and worked their way up. You cannot have nice things yet because you aren't earning big money and you will be in debt if you buy them.

BUDGET YOUR MONEY TO AVOID DEBT
You need to know how you spend it in order to save it. Buy what you need and save the rest. DO NOT buy things to impress friends. YOU NEED to SPEND LESS than WHAT YOU EARN otherwise you will go into DEBT.

DO NOT SIGN ANYTHING
Until you *FULLY UNDERSTAND* what you are signing. Do not always believe anything you are told. Find out for yourself. Take a photocopy of the document away with you to read, and ask some else's opinion *BEFORE* you sign it. Ask questions and find out what the penalties are if you don't keep the agreement.

PROTECT YOUR PERSONAL DETAILS

If anyone else gets hold of your personal information you could lose *EVERYTHING*. Be careful on websites; protect your PIN numbers; safeguard important documents and properly destroy any you no longer need; lock your mail box etc.

HAVE A DAY PLANNING SYSTEM

Using a work diary to plan your day/week, will save you time and stress.

HAVE A FILING SYSTEM

Buy a folder that has many 'pockets' and use the different pockets to store bank statements, superannuation information, work related receipts, government department information, tax returns etc. Trying to find any official paperwork or information without an organised system is going to cost you time and money.

BUILD YOUR REPUTATION, CREDIBILTY & PROFILE

Start a little earlier and stay a little later. Work smarter not harder. Do more than people expect. Give great customer service. Move on to something else when you need a bigger challenge. Always ask for a reference when you leave a job and think you have performed well.

DO A FIRST AID & C.P.R COURSE

You will have the power to save someone's life.

DONATE TIME OR MONEY TO THOSE LESS FORTUNATE

Volunteer to help the elderly, the disabled, the environment or any local organisation you have an interest in.

RETIREMENT

If you are living week to week on your wages while you are working and can't save anything, what is your life going to be like when you give up working. There is *NO* guarantee the government will continue to pay the retirement pension. Your superannuation won't be enough. *YOU* need to start saving *ASAP*. Don't think that there'll be plenty of time later because there will always be something you want to spend your money on. Get into the habit now.

LASTLY… SEEK HELP.

Life is hard and sometimes it is not fair. If you ever feel it is getting on top of you, PLEASE talk to someone…your parents, friends, or go online and find a hotline or service in your local area. Just telling someone how you are feeling can be a weight off your shoulders and they may help to get you 'back on track'.

Citations of Sources of Ideas (Bibliography)

Rules of Life; **website**; http://web.mst.edu/~adekock/Sykes-11-rules.html

Steve Jobs Explaining Success; **website**; http://thoughtcatalog.com/christopher-hudspeth/2013/08/25-wise-inspiring-steve-job-quotes-thatll-make-you-want-to-change-the-world/
by Christopher Hudspeth, posted August 17 2013

Democracy is not a spectator sport, it's a participatory event. If we don't participate in it, it ceases to be a democracy; **website**; http://www.brainyquote.com/quotes/keywords/spectator.html posted 2001-2014

The only thing necessary for the triumph of evil is for good people to do nothing; **website**; Edmund Burke. See http://quoteinvestigator.com/2010/12/04/good-men-do/

General Information; Robert Jackson quote; **website** http://usgovinfo.about.com/blquotes2.htm

Your Human Rights. website; www.samaritanmag.com Sarah Melody; We have 30 Basic Human Rights; Do you know them? updated November 16 2009 also **website**; http://www.un.org/en/documents/udhr/

Buying a Car; website; http://www.carsguide.com.au/car-advice/how-to-buy-a-used-car-10-tips-23597#.VFtq-khxnIU updated November 2014

Identity Theft; **website**; http://www.afp.gov.au/policing/fraud/identity-crime sourced February 2014

Your Mobile Phone; **website**; https://www.its.uq.edu.au/helpdesk/mobile-phone-security-tips University of Queensland updated November 2014

Tips Around the House; **Book**; Extraordinary Uses for Ordinary Things, 2009, published by Readers Digest (Australia)

Throwing Your Own Party; **website**; https://www.police.qld.gov.au/programs/cscp/personalSafety/youth/partySafe/Documents/PartySafe_HostsChecklist.pdf posted February 2014

Going to University; **website**; http://www.independent.co.uk/student/into-university/tips-for-settling-into-university-2055068.html?origin=internalSearch posted 18 August 2010

The Secrets of Successful People. Book; Sir Ray Avery, Cameron Bennett & Adrian Malloch, 2012, Random House Publishing Auckland New Zealand, **website**; http://www.fastcompany.com/3014736/how-to-be-a-success-at-everything/9-easy-to-steal-habits-of-the-super-successful Miles Kohrman July 2013 & http://addicted2success.com/success-advice/20-habits-that-will-make-you-highly-successful Chad Howse September 2013 also **website**; http://www.pickthebrain.com/blog/10-secrets-to-success/ posted January 2008 by Victor Stachura

How to Write a Good Cover Letter; **website**; http://www.roberthalf.com.au/cover-letter updated November 2014

Job Interviews; **website**; http://au.hudson.com/interview-preparation-guide & http://au.hudson.com/interview-tips-job-interview-dos-and-donts & http://au.hudson.com/interview-behavior-and-style-tips 2011-2014

Workplace Health and Safety; **Publication**; Certificate IV Occupational Health and Safety, by National Qualifications Australia, 2010 also **Publication**; Workplace Health Legislation, by National Safety Council of Australia (NSCA) 2007

The Debt Cycle. website; www.awealthofcommonsense.com Ray Dalio explains the Credit Cycle; posted 28 September 2013

Bankruptcy; **website**; http://www.moneyhelp.org.au/your-debt-options/going-bankrupt/#what-happens-to-your-assets-when-you-are-bankrupt updated November 2014

About Money. Book; 'Real Estate Mistakes' by Neil Jenman, 2000, Rowley Publications NSW Australia

About Money. website; www.kiwidebt.co.nz homepage 2011

Written Contracts; **Book**; 'Don't Sign Anything' by Neil Jenman, 2002, Rowley Publications NSW Australia

Stroke; **website**; http://www.stroke.org.nz/stroke-information 2014 & http://strokefoundation.com.au/what-is-a-stroke/signs-of-stroke/ 2014

Type II Diabetes; **website**; http://www.nlm.nih.gov/medlineplus/ency/article/000313.htm
posted June 2013 and **website**; https://www.diabetesaustralia.com.au/Documents/DA/What's%20New/12.03.14%20Diabetes%20management%20booklet%20FINAL.pdf Associate Professor Jonathan Shaw Baker IDI Heart and Diabetes Institute Australia, posted 2012 and **website**; http://www.mayoclinic.org/diseases-conditions/type-2-diabetes/basics/risk-factors/con-20031902 posted June 2014

Give Blood; **websites**; http://www.donateblood.com.au/who-can-give/am-i-eligible Australian Red Cross Blood Service also http://www.nzblood.co.nz/give-blood/donating/am-i-eligible/#.VFt5GkhxnIU
updated November 2014

Employment, Alcohol, Illicit Drugs, Girls: Book; 'Find Your Tribe' by Rebecca Sparrow, 2010, University of Queensland Press

Depression and Anxiety; **website**; http://www.beyondblue.org.au/the-facts/anxiety
http://www.beyondblue.org.au/the-facts/depression updated November 2014

Sexuality Confusion. Book; 'How To Talk To Girls' (Chapter 8 Same-Sex Attracted Teens)by Jonathan Roussaint, 2011, Allen & Unwin Sydney, Melbourne.

Stages of Grief When Dealing with Loss; **website**; http://www.recover-from-grief.com/7-stages-of-grief.html accessed November 2014

Domestic Violence; **website**; http://www.dvrcv.org.au/national-sexual-assault-family-domestic-violence-counselling-line sourced February 2013

Travel. Pocketbook; 'Before you go...Stop' by New Zealand Government, Ministry of Foreign Affairs and Trade also **website**; http://www.nzembassy.com/australia/new-zealanders-overseas/safe-travel accessed November 2014

Cashback Schemes; **website**; http://www.choice.com.au/reviews-and-tests/money/shopping-and-legal/shopping/cashback-capers/page/how%20it%20works%20and%20traps.aspx posted Dec 2008

Thanks to Lisa Lyford; Girls (10 Wardrobe Essentials Every Woman Should Own) for her copyright permission.

NOTES

NOTES

NOTES

NOTES

NOTES

NOTES

NOTES

NOTES

NOTES

NOTES

NOTES

NOTES